Charlie Crowe's Newcastle United Scrapbook

Edited by

Mike Kirkup

Newcastle's official mascot, Peter Anderson of Byker, in striped suit, accompanies the 1952 squad on their triumphant tour of the city with the FA Cup from the Central Station to St James' Park.

Previous page: Charlie Crowe heads for goal against Tottenham in 1950. United won 7-0.

Copyright © Charlie Crowe & Mike Kirkup 2009

First published in 2001

Reprinted in 2009 by

The Charlie Crowe Appeal
Newcastle Healthcare Charity
Room 203, Cheviot Court
Heaton
Newcastle upon Tyne
NE7 7DN

Registered Charity Number 502473

ISBN 978-1-906721-09-1

Contents

Cramlington-born Tommy Walker (left) crosses the ball as Len Shackleton (right) looks on against Bradford Park Avenue in 1947.

Foreword

Charlie Crowe will always be remembered as a hero of Newcastle United's three successful FA Cup campaigns in the 1950s, and I personally saw them all. His 'Scrapbook' is a great collection of pictures and stories, but it also shows Charlie as we remember him – a great guy, steadfast and kind. True to form, he donated to charity all the proceeds of his books and talks. The first edition of this book raised much needed money for the Jackie Milburn Fund, so typical of Charlie.

Now Charlie is the last man alive from the glory squad of the 1950s. Unfortunately he is now suffering from Alzheimer's disease – a terrible affliction. His response is to get down to work and do something about it. The proceeds of this book will go entirely to help medical research by raising money to buy a new research scanner for the Newcastle Magnetic Resonance Centre.

Football is a passion in the North East. But we are also passionate about people. Charlie's efforts both on and off the pitch reflect this. I thoroughly endorse the Charlie Crowe Scanner Appeal.

Bobby Robson
January 2009

Charlie Crowe shakes the hand of King George VI before the 1951 FA Cup Final at Wembley.

Charlie Crowe Scanner Appeal

The proceeds of this book go to The Charlie Crowe Appeal. The appeal has been launched to raise money for a new research scanner at the Newcastle University Magnetic Resonance Centre on the Campus for Ageing and Vitality.

Charlie Crowe now has Alzheimer's disease. This terrible affliction is the focus of groundbreaking research involving both local people with the disease and healthy volunteers. It is a major part of the work of the Magnetic Resonance Centre which also researches diabetes and other chronic conditions.

Visit the website charliecroweappeal.com
for more information about Charlie and the research.

The appeal operates in association with the
Newcastle Healthcare Charity (registered charity number 502473)
Room 203, Cheviot Court, Heaton, Newcastle upon Tyne, NE7 7DN.
Telephone No: 0191 2231434.

The Glory Days

For Newcastle United the outbreak of the Second World War meant a breathing space which was to revitalise the club. As Hitler's invading masses spread across Europe, United were at their lowest ebb, but by the time the darkness of a bloody confrontation was behind us, the black and whites were ready for a glorious drive to the very top.

Season 1937/38 had seen United plummet to the very depths. They avoided relegation to the Third Division North by one-tenth of a goal, finishing on the same points as Barnsley who went down. (In those days it was goal average not goal difference or goals scored.) Never before had United suffered such humiliation. But in their darkest hour came a man who was to lead them out of the wilderness ... Stan Seymour.

The little Geordie, a Cup winner in 1924 and a vital part of the 1927 side which won the First Division Championship, had been shunned by United after leaving the club in bitterness. But during the summer of 1938 Seymour was unexpectedly offered a seat on the United board after the shock fear of relegation from the Second Division. It was to prove a turning point.

The last full season before War was declared, 1938/39, saw United gain some respectabilty. In fact at one stage – as the new year dawned – they lay in second position, but injuries crippled their promotion aspirations.

The shining lights then at St James' were Ray Bowden, a fine creator, and defender Jimmy Denmark, but a significant figure emerged from the reserves – striker Albert Stubbins who was to produce a shoal of wartime goals.

After only three Second Division games of 1939/40, Hitler's brutality brought down the curtain on League football. United had lost their first two away fixtures at Millwall and Nottingham Forest without scoring a goal, but signed off with a bang, slaughtering Swansea 8-1 at St James' Park.

It was during these war years that Seymour refashioned United. While a lot of clubs waited for their stars to return as veterans, Seymour wisely scoured the North East for fresh young talent. The likes of Jackie Milburn, Charlie Wayman, Bobby Cowell, Doug Graham, George Hair, George Stobbart, Ernie Taylor and Charlie Crowe joined United, and with Seymour also buying well to bring in Frank Brennan, Joe Harvey and Roy Bentley the stage was set for promotion from the Second Division and the ultimate glory of winning the FA Cup three times in the space of five years in the early '50s.

And those Glory Days of the 1950s are covered comprehensively in the following pages, using the unique personal voice and scrapbooks of Charlie Crowe, plus articles gleaned from the sports' pages of practically every local and national newspaper in the land.

Mike Kirkup

'THE FA CUP AND ME IT'S LIKE MEETING AN OLD FRIEND'

It's difficult to say who was more proud, me or my father, Charles, when I showed off the FA Cup at a presentation at Heaton RAOB Club.

After the Magpies' Wembley win in 1951, I managed to keep the FA Cup to myself for a whole fortnight. I had gone to the office at St James' and asked if I could borrow it. They thought I would bring it back after an hour or two, so I was told that would be OK. In effect, I took it all over the place.

During that time, I got a phone call from Hughie Gallacher, a Newcastle United legend from the 1920s. He asked if I would take the Cup over to a club at Pelaw near Gateshead. This was against club policy as it wasn't covered by insurance.

This photo of me and Hughie with the Cup appeared in a local paper and I was summoned before my betters to give an account of why the coveted silverware had gone walkabouts round the pubs and clubs of the Tyne. But almost fifty years later in October 2000 I was able to show off the Cup, this time legitimately, in a car showroom near where I live now at

It was a pleasure to show off the Cup to Hughie Gallacher, one of United's all-time greats.

This shows me on the right with Lawrie Good, an executive with AXA, the present FA Cup sponsors.

Benton. A kind-hearted motor dealer, John Pearson, had paid £1,000 to St Oswald's Hospice for the honour of showing off the trophy and charging people to have their photos taken with the Cup in his car showroom, all for charity.

That day I thought I had met up again with an old friend, 'cos that was what the FA Cup was to Newcastle United in the 1950s – after all, we did win it three years out of five!

It was during that time that they kept calling Newcastle 'a Cup team'. Well, I don't know about that, but, in the 1950s, Newcastle had a lot of players who raised their game for one-off occasions. In 1951 we should have been the first club to do the Double in the twentieth century. Between the semi and the Final we played about ten League matches and never won one, but still finished about fourth in the League.

The Football Association Challenge Cup was the attraction, you see. The League was mundane, your bread-and-butter stuff. There was no real incentive for us in the League: there was no European Cup; the glamour was at Wembley and so were the cash bonuses. Not that we got all that much – in 1951 the bandsmen of the Coldstream Guards got more money for playing at Wembley in the Cup Final than we did. Jackie Milburn reckoned it up many years later, and he says for winning *three* FA Cup-winners medals (which he did with Bob Cowell and Bob Mitchell), he received a grand total of £73-16d-0d!

The '51 team got on really well together. During any match, I had little Ernie Taylor always available in

Jackie Milburn stayed with Newcastle until 1957 when he left to be player/coach of Irish team, Linfield.

the centre of the park. You might play a one-two with him and he'd set off speedsters in the front line, Jackie Milburn and Tommy Walker. Behind them we had Joe Harvey who took no prisoners, and Bob Cowell. On my side of the field we had Bobby Mitchell, and then there was George Robledo who was the poacher. George would make for the far post as soon as Mitch got the ball. And those were our attacking moves: simple, really, but we had two centre-forwards before anybody else thought of doing it.

'Local boy makes good', how I used to thrill when as a teenager I read of a young player succeeding in a football team with his home town club. Reading about it was wonderful, but nothing like so good as accomplishing it myself – particularly when supporters know how to appreciate the success of a lad from around the corner, as do the folk who follow Newcastle United.

In those days the players had a rapport with the fans. We weren't all that far removed from the shipbuilders, the miners and the steel workers. Before I became a pro footballer I served my apprenticeship at Parsons, then after the war started I moved to Burradon Colliery. I was playing in the first-team for United then, but one day I hurt my finger at work. Word got around at Burradon and this very well-spoken NCB manager walked into the pit canteen one day and asked: 'Is Charlie Crowe in here?' I replied that I was he, and he said: 'How is your finger, Charlie?' I told him it was fine and he seemed relieved. A few weeks later I went to take a throw-in at St James' and this wag in the crowd shouted: 'Hey, Charlie ... hoo's ya finger?' After that it became something of a catchphrase. That's how close the players were to the supporters.

The Geordie fans have had their fair share of costly stars over the years, yet they have never allowed themselves to become obsessed by transfer fees. On Tyneside, they appreciate good football, no matter who plays it. And in the 1940s and '50s, whatever you cost the club – £10 or £25,000 – the miners and shipyard workers then, and others who wore the black and white emblem would always give their support, 'cos they have a great understanding of their football. Their cheers were a great spur to me.

Two games in particular stand out – a remarkable match against Stoke City with Stan Matthews, and the day I helped Newcastle to beat Blackpool and win the FA Cup in 1951.

1951 wasn't to be Stan Matthews' year.

I came into football the way most others did in those days: through the junior game. And it was after one of those games that our boss then, Stan Seymour, signed me. And so, at seventeen years of age, I found myself playing for the team I had previously supported – loudly – from the terraces.

At that time, Newcastle had a great player and skipper called Harry Clifton who was a father-figure to young lads like myself, Bob Cowell, Bob Corbett, George Hair, Tommy Thompson, Andy Graver and Ernie Taylor.

Many years later, the Jackie Milburn Trust Fund presented Harry Clifton with a signed photo of himself leading out a United team in 1943 that included Albert Stubbins, George Wayman, Bob Cowell and Jackie Milburn.

I hadn't been playing all that long in the first team when Stoke City visited us. Opposing me was Stan Matthews, a player whose pictures I had stuck in my album and whom I had worshipped from afar. In the past I had seen him, a smiling modest chap, leaving the ground after a super display. He was a legend to me. But this afternoon the legend was a fact, and I was the left-half opposing him, trying with my full-back to form a plan that would bring us partial success.

Frankly, I walked out on the field in a flat spin and came off in one. But the cheers were ringing in my ears, and Matthews' congratulatory arm was round my shoulder.

Everyone thought I had a good game. Newcastle dictated the play to pull off a terrific 9-1 win. Later, I had another memorable game against Stan in a Cup Final, but first came a few seasons of mixed fortunes. When Dougie Wright returned to the club, I stepped down into the reserves, but lapped up all the instructions he provided. England had many fine wing-halves in those days, such as Billy Wright etc, but I unhesitatly put Dougie as the best of them. His talents should have earned him much more fame

Anyway, when it seemed I had a chance of promotion into the first squad, a broken ankle put me out of the game. For a long time I could never recover my confidence and was completely out of touch.

Doug Wright is seen 3rd right at back in a 1947 team. Back left: Frank Watts (secretary), Joe Harvey, Ben Craig, Eric Garbutt, Bob Corbett, Doug Wright, Norman Smith (trainer) and Stan Seymour (then honorary manager). Front: Jack Milburn, Jim Woodburn, George King, Charlie Wayman, Tom Pearson and Frank Brennan.

At Glasgow in 1945 where United were playing in a tournament. Left to right: George Hair, me and Paddy Woods.

In our promotion year of 1948, I got only a couple of games; the following season more injuries hit me. Not once was I in the first team, and my morale was at its lowest. In 1948, after Newcastle's promotion, I went with the team on a short tour of Ireland. One night at our hotel I had reason to ask Stan Seymour for some cash for expenses, and he referred me to club secretary, Frank Watt Jnr, who was still in his bedroom. I knocked on his door and a faint voice called: 'Come in. What is it you want?' I explained to the secretary who was still in bed. He said: 'OK, Charlie, if you just reach my socks over, I'll give you the money.' A pair of black socks were draped over the board at the bottom of the bed ... they were stuffed with pound notes – that's where he kept all of Newcastle United's petty cash.

This shows us in Ballymena. From left: Frank Watt, Eric Garbutt, Bob Stokoe, me, Andy Donaldson, Norman Dodgin, Ernie Taylor, Tom Walker and Joe Sibley.

There was still an Irish connection on 17th September 1949 when two newcomers made their debut against Manchester City. I shall let Alf McMichael explain how that came about:

'George Hannah and I caught the ferry from Belfast and got the train from Stranraer. It was a Saturday, our first day at Newcastle, fresh from Irish League football with Linfield and neither of us dreamed we'd be playing that afternoon. We were met at Newcastle's Central Station by the manager George Martin and taken to the old Station Hotel where United often had lunch on match days.

'We met the other lads and that's when they dropped the bombshell that we were playing that afternoon. I was 21-years-old with George about the same, and even though we were used to playing in front of crowds of 16,000 at Linfield, we were not prepared for anything like St James' Park. It was a huge jump, but all the more so for being informed at the last minute.

'It was a brilliant game, and we ran out 4-2 winners with my mate George Hannah getting one of the goals. In fact, George had an excellent game, but when I spoke to people afterwards they would say: "Hang on a minute – you didn't do too bad yourself – you have a great future."

Alf McMichael was United's most capped player.

OFF ON THE ROAD TO WEMBLEY, 1950/51

It was in 1950 that I became established in the first team.

In 1950, I returned to the senior side. When I got into the team it was just blending together and twelve months later we began our Cup travels. Our first game of the new season, as luck had it, was against Stoke City, the team I had made my debut against. Jackie Milburn was in fine form after his trip to Rio with the England World Cup squad. He whizzed around a Stoke defence that was missing their international centre-half Neil Franklin who had absconded to Bogota, to score after a typical raking run. Later Jackie put the game beyond Stoke's reach with a penalty.

But Jackie was injured and not present in this particular United squad that was described in a Liverpool programme at Anfield, early in 1950:

GARBUTT Eric (goalkeeper). This talented young Scarborough-born goalkeeper joined Newcastle from Billingham Synthonia in 1939. Reliable deputy for Jack Fairbrother. Stands 5ft 10ins and weighs 10st 2lbs.

COWELL Robert (right-back). One of the few United players who did not cost a penny piece. He played for a number of his local Tyneside junior teams before United took him on the St James' staff in 1943. A tenacious defender who really came into his own last season when he made 38 first-team appearances.

McMICHAEL Alfred (left-back). A newcomer to the Newcastle ranks, he joined them only a few weeks ago with ex-Evertonian George Hannah. Is gradually settling down to the tremendous pace of English football, and manager George Martin believes he will prove a real winner.

HARVEY Joseph (right-half). Tall, strongly built, native of Doncaster who keeps up a remarkable pace throughout the 90 minutes. It was in November 1936 that he went to Wolves from Edlington Rangers. April the following year saw him move to Bournemouth, then on to Bradford City in August 1938. After seven years with the City, he was bought by Newcastle at a cost of £4,250 in October 1945. Present captain.

Bobby Cowell was a Durham lad, born at Trimdon Colliery. He could be relied upon to make last ditch saves on the line when his 'keeper was beaten. He was one of only a trio of United players who won all three cupwinners' medals in the 1950s – the other two were Mitchell and Milburn.

BRENNAN Frank (centre-half). Dominating Scotsman who is the sheet-anchor of the United defensive set-up. Is 6ft 2ins and rose from Scottish junior football to international rank in five seasons. Airdrieonians spotted him playing with Coatbridge St Joseph's when he was only fifteen. Airdrie received the handsome sum of £8,000 when they transferred him to Newcastle United in May 1946. He played in every match during Newcastle's promotion season (1948) and missed only one game last year.

CROWE Charles (left-half). Originally a right-half, he is a local wartime signing from Walker-on-Tyne. An indefatigable worker with the emphasis on attack, he recently made the first-team grade. Was on the transfer list at the beginning of the season, but he is now finally re-established.

WALKER Thomas (outside-right). Another Tyneside junior find who cost the club nothing in transfer fees. Walker is exceptionally fast and always a dangerous raider. Scored five goals in 22 appearances last season. He joined United from his local Cramlington in 1941.

THOMPSON Thomas (inside-right). A lightly-built youngster who came from Lumley Juniors, Co. Durham, just after the war. More of a schemer than an effective marksman, he had his senior baptism in February 1949. Has also appeared at outside-right.

ROBLEDO George (centre-forward). Former Barnsley centre-forward who comes of a Chilean father and a Yorkshire mother. Has been in England since he was six. George and his brother Ted cost Newcastle a round sum of £25,000 when they were taken from Barnsley last February. Had trials with Huddersfield in schools' football.

HANNAH George (inside-left). Merseyside-born youngster with clever football ideas. Signed for Everton at fifteen, and later gained his place in the Liverpool FA Youths' eleven. Served in Ireland with the Army and was allowed by Everton to play with Linfield for whom he signed as professional when he was demobbed.

MITCHELL Robert (outside-left). A six-footer who has proved one of Newcastle's best Scottish buys. It was in 1943 that he joined Third Lanark from Market Star, a Scottish juvenile side. After six seasons with 'Third' he joined United in February this year, and he cost nearly £20,000. Possessor of a tremendous left-foot shot which he used to effect against Everton at St James' Park earlier this season.

George Hannah scored on his debut against Manchester City.

HOUGHTON Frank (inside-left) Normally a wing half-back, but has recently been doing well in the inside-forward position. A native of Preston, he was playing for the Irish club Ballymena when United secured him about two years ago. Played a vital role in gaining Newcastle promotion against Sheffield Wednesday, and broke an arm in the process.

We had begun the 1950/51 season in fine fettle, and this victory over Stoke City began a record-breaking run of ten games without defeat. This is how the *Newcastle Journal* man Ken McKenzie saw that game:

'After Stoke City had thrice gone within inches of scoring inside 12 minutes, Newcastle led 3-0 in 27 minutes in the opening Football League game of the season at St James' Park, and added three goals between the 77th and 84th minutes to win 6-0.

'Those early Stoke near-misses, which might well have left United with a big task to cancel the effect of poor marking and some unhappy goalkeeping by Stoke 'keeper Herod when Newcastle got going in attack, must have

This 1950 squad photo was taken in civvies with a few lads wearing their Newcastle blazers. From back left: Tom Walker, George Hannah, Bob Corbett, Bob Cowell, Ron Batty and George Robledo. Front: Frank Brennan, Bob Stokoe, Jack Fairbrother, Jack Milburn, Charlie Crowe and Bob Mitchell.

well-nigh broken Stoke's hearts. Any remaining Stoke hope faded in the interval when it was stated that the City centre-half Frank Mountford appeared to have broken his jaw during early play.

'Mountford insisted on resuming on the left wing, but Stoke were in no position to recover from such a load of trouble. Scoring sequence in a game equalling that at home against Huddersfield last season, the most clear-cut success by United in post-war First Division football, was Robledo 6 mins; Crowe 22; Milburn 27 and 77; Mitchell 81; and Milburn 86.'

Milburn scored the two goals which beat Burnley 2-1; we swamped Huddersfield 6-0; in a top-of-the-table tussle, Arsenal, under skipper Joe Mercer, were beaten 2-1; and so it went on. The Magpies were sitting pretty, and there didn't seem to be another team around in the First Division to knock us off our perch. The team were blending well, Fairbrother was now established in goal and proved an invaluable last line of defence.

Milburn later wrote a book called *Golden Goals*. In it he said:

'Jack Fairbrother was the finest goalkeeper I ever saw in my life. Typical of him was when he used to ask me to go back two or three afternoons a week with him to train. And, mind, Jack, when he came to Newcastle, was twenty-eight or something and he was thirty-one when he left, I think.

'Him and I used to go to St James' Park, and he had two long ropes on the goalposts. He used to have me running in from various angles, and I used to come running up, and he would shout "STOP!" I would be tearing in, and as soon as he shouted I put my foot on the ball and kept running out of the road, so the ball was left at an angle where he was in comparison with the posts. I used to run straight on, and Jack never moved. The ball was left there, and we'd get the rope from one post to the ball, and the other post to the ball, and if Jack wasn't in the centre of that rope we had to do it over and over again until he got it to perfection. And this took hours. He was an "angle" goalkeeper.

'Ronnie Simpson was brilliant, but he was a goal-line goalie. Relied on reflexes. But Jack was just the opposite. As a forward on the field, whenever the opposition press your goal, you sometimes get a sinking feeling because you know they're going to score. You never had that feeling with Fairbrother.

Fairbrother was an 'angle' goalkeeper.

'As soon as Jack Fairbrother started coming away from the line we knew that his angle was right. We weren't always right, but you never had the feeling that you were going to lose.'

It is not all that well known, but George Robledo, above, took part in the 1950 World Cup at Rio when he played for Chile.

George Robledo was proving to be an excellent buy from Barnsley, and profiting a great deal from being Milburn's back-up man. Frank Brennan was later to say:

'George was doing great, knocking in hat-tricks all over the place. But most of them were put down to Milburn. Jackie would have a crack ... aye, from twenty or thirty yards, and they would come off the woodwork or a defender's body, and there would be George to put them away. He was always poaching around the goal-mouth.

'We were talking about a particular incident in our penalty area after one game, and George pipes up with: "I didn't know *that* happened!" And Joe Harvey barks at him: "George, how the hell would you know what happens in our goal-mouth – you never come into our half of the bloody field!"

Joe Harvey's attitude and actions on the field were often down-to-earth. If the only way to stop an opponent was to bring him down, then down he came. If the only way to motivate a player was to curse him, then he had the language for the occasion. The rest of the side had a lot to thank him for as United set about taking the world of football apart in that 1950/51 season.

Again Milburn wrote:

'I'll tell you why I admired Joe Harvey. He wasn't a good player, and he used to get more bollockings off the crowd than cheers. But even so, I couldn't understand how a man could get that kind of stick off the crowd and still guide a team the way he did. In other words, he forgot what the crowd was saying. He still kept at us: "You bloody well do this ..." and such, even though he was having a stinker! It takes a good man to do that. I couldn't understand how a man could do it. Because if the crowd began to get at me, I used to go into me shell.

'At school, with being sports champion, a lot of people looked up to you in the class, and it made you feel good. I'd never had that before – never had any bollockings. And when it did happen, you didn't know how to react. I would rather have gone into me shell and hid somewhere or pretended I was injured. And yet he shrugged the whole lot off, and said "Bugger them!" to guide the team. It takes guts. He was an extraordinary character, was Joe.

'People have often asked me if I'd like to be playing now (1988) with all the big money that's floating around. I know the money would have been nice, but if it meant missing playing with the lads that we had at St James' just after the war – the Brennans, Cowells, Harveys, Crowes and Mitchells – whey man, there's no way I would ever have missed that. It was a laugh a minute with the lads. The likes of Jack Fairbrother ... they were so dedicated. There's no money would ever have been able to buy that team.'

That 1950s squad had been built around some good local lads who are seen in these 1945 photos of a game against Everton. From left: Bob Corbett, me, Harry Catterick of Everton, Joe Harvey and Tot Smith.

Me, Wainwright of Everton and Tot Smith.

Midway through that season, the team affairs were taken over again by Stan Seymour, with George Martin leaving Newcastle to take up a similar position with Aston Villa. Martin, although being in charge of Newcastle's promotion-winning side of 1948, had never enjoyed full control over either team selection or tactics. A typical Martin team-talk went like this:

To Jack Fairbrother: 'Jack ... the 18-yard area ... make it your own. You're the boss!'

To Cowell and Corbett: 'Now ... the two Bobs ... these two wingers ... put a rope around their necks!'

To Joe Harvey: 'Joe ... keep 'em going!'

To Frank Brennan: 'Frank ... put 'em in your pocket!'

To me: 'Charlie ... give them the usual!' (Bashing one fist against the other.)

To Walker and Milburn: 'Tom ... Jackie ... show 'em your arses!'

To Ernie Taylor: (Ruffling Ernie's hair) 'Aha! ... The little man!' (Nodding his head as if to emphasise the point.)

To George Robledo: 'George ... the far post!'

To Bobby Mitchell: 'Mitch ... that extra man ... don't overdo it!'

Right then, lads – out you go!

We kept on piling up the points and were well in contention with Arsenal, the League leaders, when we went to White Hart Lane to take on newly promoted Tottenham. But Spurs put a stop to our gallop, flashing seven goals past a bewildered Fairbrother who was getting the angles wrong for once, in front of a colossal 70,000 crowd, to go top of the League.

The FA Cup got under way, with the lads easily disposing of Second Division Bury 4-1. Fourth Round opponents Bolton Wanderers proved far more difficult, even at St James' Park. Bobby Mitchell got United's head in front after

'Wor Jackie' scoring against Bury and setting United off on the road to Wembley.

only four minutes, to send a 67,596 crowd wild, but a defence without big Frank Brennan was always going to find Nat Lofthouse a handful. Brennan's deputy, McNeil, was panicked into giving away a needless free kick just outside the Newcastle penalty area. From the resulting melée Moir headed an equaliser. Mattie McNeil began scything Lofthouse to the ground at every opportunity. During a lull in the game Nat asked me: 'Who the hell is this fella? Does he think he's playing rugby, or what? He'd better watch himself of I'll have him.'

Just before half-time Lofthouse and McNeil clashed again in a grinding tackle that left the Newcastle player flat out on the ground. As Norman Smith was giving him treatment, the big centre-half was yelling across at Lofthouse what he'd do to him when he got back on his feet. Nat strode across, and with a voice full of menace said: 'Lad, you're not going to get up again: you're out of the match.' The Bolton player was right, and McNeil, from then on, was a virtual passenger on the wing.

Lofthouse, now with acres of space, laid on another goal for Moir, and we found ourselves behind in a game that we had completely dominated from the first whistle.

The game was held up for five minutes while the police cleared the

Nat Lofthouse's brave performances for England earned him the nickname 'Lion of Vienna'.

field of jubilant Lancashire fans. But if the Bolton supporters thought it was all over, they had reckoned without Milburn. Standing almost nonchalantly with his face to his own goal, Jackie received the ball, swivelled on his heel, and shot the ball past Hanson before the goalie even sensed there was any danger. This was the drama of a man who could turn defeat into victory in an instant. Minutes later, as an immobile Bolton defence stood appealing for offside, Milburn walked the ball through into the net to put our Newcastle marble into the bag for the next round.

In the Fifth Round we proved far too good for Stoke City at the Victoria Ground, winning easily 4-2 with Robledo scoring twice. Brennan returned for this game to stiffen United's defence. Near neighbours Sunderland were also through, but in a thrilling replay went out to Wolverhampton Wanderers, defeated 3-1. Newcastle's next Cup-tie also went to a replay, as we were held to a goalless draw at home by Third Division Bristol Rovers.

The game at Eastville proved less difficult (they even put Jackie Milburn's face at the front of their programme) and goals from Taylor, Crowe and Milburn were enough to scupper the Pirates 3-1.

Eager ears listened for the semi-final draw at lunch-time the following Monday. Newcastle's opponents would be either Birmingham, Blackpool or Wolves. Of the three, we would probably have preferred Birmingham or Blackpool. We were drawn against Billy Wright's Wolves.

Joe Harvey, surely tempting fate, wrote the following article for the *Newcastle Journal*, printed on the morning of the match. It was headed – 'Next Stop Wembley!'

F.A. CUP SIXTH ROUND (RE-PLAY)

BRISTOL ROVERS
VERSUS
NEWCASTLE UNITED
Played at EASTVILLE STADIUM, BRISTOL on WEDNESDAY, FEBRUARY 28th, 1951

JACKIE MILBURN
(England and Newcastle F.C.)

PHOTOGRAPHIC SOUVENIR PROGRAMME   SIXPENCE

'Wembley – here comes Newcastle United! That heartfelt wish just about covers the range of my hope and determination this morning. As I have been disappointed in one semi-final since the war, this game means a great deal to me.

'Why does the Cup bite so deep? It's not the brass, though I'm six foot of Yorkshire in that sort of collecting. We all know the League is the real test. In the next couple of months United will pull out their last reserves for the Championship run in. But the Cup? Well, it's an adventure.

'And when you get there? How should I know? I've only seen Wembley stands rising in the distance when travelling, and gazed longingly at the ground itself at the cinema.

'And now we are nearly tossing a coin for the lucky dressing-room. I cannot get my thoughts past that ... WEMBLEY, HERE WE COME!'

CUP-TIE SCENE at Hillsborough, Sheffield, yesterday, when a section of the crowd came over the barrier and invaded the pitch. Ambulance men were soon busy with fainting cases, and after order was restored the duel between Newcastle United and Wolverhampton continued.

NOT A GOAL WAS SCORED,
AND STILL NO ONE KNOWS WHO'LL
GO TO WEMBLEY

NEWCASTLE United, after a hard-fought goal-less draw with Wolverhampton Wanderers in the semi-final of the F.A. Cup at Sheffield yesterday, have to go through it all again at Huddersfield on Wednesday.

The other semi-final, between Blackpool and Birmingham at Manchester, was also goalless, and will be replayed on Wednesday at Goodison Park, Everton.

St. John Ambulance men dealt with more than 200 fainting cases at the Sheffield game. At the start of the game a spectator collapsed and died from heart failure.

.. First come, first served is the policy for obtaining tickets for the Huddersfield replay. An all ticket match has been ruled out, but a limit of 50,000 has been placed on the ground.

A small number of stand seats will be available, however, and an announcement of detailed arrangements will be made later.

The new stand has seating accommodation for more than 4,000.

One third of the tickets are to be sold at Huddersfield and the remainder equally divided between Newcastle and Wolves.

Huddersfield start selling their share of stand and paddock tickets at 10 a.m. today until 4 p.m. Any tickets left over will be sold on Monday and Tuesday.

Price of admission to the ground is 2s. 6d. Other prices are: Centre stand £1 1s., stands B and D 10s. 6d., stands A and E 7s., paddock 3s. 6d.

EXCURSION PLANS

Mr. G. B. Gray, District Passenger Manager, British Railways, told "The Sunday Sun" that probably five excursion trains would leave the Central Station, Newcastle, on Wednesday between about 6.30 a.m. and 10.30 a.m. The last two would have restaurant cars and the return fare would be 17s. 6d.

The District Passenger Manager's office will be open today at the Central Station between 10 a.m. and noon for party bookings. No individual bookings will be taken.

The team are to stay at Buxton —their present headquarters— until after the replay.

"The lads would have got a rousing reception on their arrival home for putting up such a magnificent display at Sheffield," a disappointed supporter told "The Sunday Sun."

The 20,000 Newcastle United supporters pouring out of Hillsborough Ground, Sheffield, at 4.45 yesterday were of one mind—"Let's get on to Huddersfield."

There was almost a disaster at Hillsborough in 1951 when United played their semi-final against Wolves. It says in the caption that spectators 'invaded the pitch', however, it is more likely that the fans at the front were forced on to the pitch due to pressure at the back. The identical circumstances that claimed almost 100 lives at the same ground in 1989.

Mr. Stan Seymour, Newcastle's director who is acting as manager, said: "We ought, on the balance of play, to have won but it is a fair result. It would, I think, have been an injustice if either side had scored."

Mr. Seymour was certain that whichever team won this semi-final would win the Cup.

Wolves' manager, Stan. Cullis, watched the game from the trainers' box.

Mr. Cullis' verdict: "It was a hard fight."

Many Newcastle supporters spent over five hours in the ground.

Newcastle played Wolves at Sheffield's Hillsborough ground, and the other two teams met at Maine Road, Manchester. For the first time since 1912, both semi-finals ended as draws – and goalless draws at that. Two would-be England centre-forwards were on view at Hillsborough: Newcastle's Milburn and Roy Swinbourne of Wolves. Both had the ball in the net in the first five minutes but their efforts were disallowed, Milburn's for 'offside' and Swinbourne's for 'hand-ball'.

The Newcastle v Wolves replay was arranged for Huddersfield, and the other game was scheduled for Goodison Park, home of Everton. Wolves' team for that game on 14th March 1951 was: Williams, Short, Pritchard, Russell, Shorthouse, Wright, Hancocks, Walker, Swinbourne, Dunn and Mullen. The Newcastle side was: Fairbrother, Cowell, Corbett, Harvey, Brennan, Crowe, Walker, Taylor, Milburn, Robledo and Mitchell.

For a long time that day it was doubtful whether the match would get under way. Incessant rain had flooded the pitch and terraces, and huge pipes were brought in to pump out the water. Minutes before the kick-off the referee declared the pitch fit, but there was no time to clear away the metal pipes so they were stacked behind the goals.

Wolves shocked us and the thousands of United's travelling fans by scoring an early goal through inside-right Walker. Now under extreme pressure, Corbett gave away a corner on the left which was quickly taken by Wolves' England winger, Hancocks. Big Frank Brennan rose above the Wolves' attack to head clear, but in doing so stumbled and fell off the field, banging his head against a metal pipe. Stan Seymour swore he heard the crack up in the directors' box.

Norman Smith raced on to the pitch to where Harvey was bending over the motionless Brennan, whose face had by now turned ashen grey. Joe turned around and said, 'My God! He's got to be dead.'

Smith produced the magic sponge and Brennan rose shakily to his feet, eyes rolling around in his head. Harvey pleaded with the trainer to pull him around.

A little colour seeped back into Frank's craggy face, and Smith held up two fingers: 'Frank, how many fingers have I got up?' The Scot mumbled and swayed, but said nothing. Brennan got a little more coherent, and the referee, eager to get the game away after such a long stoppage, waved our trainer from the field. As he was running off, Smith turned to Brennan and shouted: 'For heaven's sake, Frank, let your head clear before you attempt to head the ball again.' Brennan nodded, but in Wolves' very next attack he met a vicious drive square on the forehead, and the ball flew thirty yards upfield. We Newcastle players held our breath, expecting Frank to topple once again, but he just grinned as we looked on in astonishment.

Norman Smith – whose Newcastle United connections covered four decades.

The game was another personal triumph for Jackie Milburn. Newcastle refused to be flustered by that early Wolves goal, and Jackie had a simple tap-in after a piece of Taylor magic had opened up the Wolves defence. Minutes later it was Milburn's turn to do the donkey work and leave the rest to the sweet left foot of Bobby Mitchell. Joe Harvey's perilous prediction had come true. Wembley, here we come!

That win put Newcastle United into the Cup Final for the eighth time. We had been the bookies' favourites for a long time to lift the trophy, and were very well placed to do the 'Double'. Immediately after the final whistle had blown after the replay victory, Seymour raced into the Newcastle dressing room, threw his arms around each player in turn and announced: 'Thank you, everybody! It was a wonderful performance, and I'll tell you all straight away, there's going to be no worrying about who plays in the Cup Final. Whatever happens, you fellows who've brought us this far will play at Wembley.'

Unbelievable! There were still nine matches to be played in the League, and United had to win only about half of them to win the championship. Yet the Newcastle manager had handed the players what amounted to a free hand in the way they would approach the remaining games. Milburn wrote:

'It was during this pre-Final period that I realised what a tremendous strain was being placed upon the men due to play at Wembley. Although none of us ever thought of holding back from a tackle for fear of being hurt, or taking a chance which may have brought us an injury, I'm confident that, quite unconsciously, every man who is going to play in a great match doesn't put everything he possesses into ordinary League games before the great day.

'For the next six weeks our Newcastle team tottered from one defeat to the next, disappointing the worried followers and causing the bookies to install opponents Blackpool, who had seen off Birmingham, as new favourites to win the Cup. The match was now being hailed as the 'Matthews Final', with every neutral football fan in the country hoping that Stan, now approaching forty years of age, would get the one honour that had eluded him for so long.'

Four weeks before the Wembley game, the teams met in a dress rehearsal at Bloomfield Road. Blackpool, mid-placed in the League, rested Matthews and Perry. We played without Ernie Taylor and Joe Harvey. Blackpool inside-forward Alan Brown, who was to break a leg in a later game and so miss Wembley, was prominent with long, strength-sapping runs through the mud and water that clogged up the middle of the pitch. It was from one of these runs that the first Blackpool goal was scored through Mortenson: a great header stemming from a prodigious leap.

Milburn gave goalie Farm an ominous taste of what was to come at Wembley by firing in the equaliser with a twenty-five-yard oblique shot. Only seconds later Mudie put Blackpool ahead, again from a Wardle centre. Bob Stokoe, getting a rare game in Harvey's absence, kicked into an open space

Mortenson in an England shirt being tackled by Scotland's George Young. You can spot Milburn under Stan's armpit!.

for Robledo to run on and level the scores once again. The match ended that way – 2-2 – and a report in the *Sunday Pictorial* ended with:

'If these two teams can produce at Wembley the same quality of football as on this occasion under such adverse conditions, it augurs well for a great Final.'

A week before the Final was due to be played, the United team and directors headed for the beneficial Spa waters of Buxton. The team had used the Derbyshire town before for special training, and it had got to be a lucky hideout for us, with United always winning big matches after staying there. Team talks from trainer Smith and manager Seymour tended to be short and to the point. No blackboards here with pin-men moved around like robots; this was the era of 'gut' football. We as players felt instinctively what was the right thing to do. The advent of the all-knowing soccer coach had not yet made inroads into what was a rousing game, exciting to watch, and a thrilling spectacle which still pulled in massive crowds in all kinds of weather.

Coaching was looked upon as something of a joke by the long-serving pros. Walter Winterbottom had been giving an England side some slide-rule advice, and ended with: 'When it's on, I want Wright to transfer the ball to Finney, then Finney to Mannion. Mullen and Milburn will then go on dummy runs, and the ball will be switched back to Finney who will get to the bye-line and cross for Shackleton who will put it into the net.' Biding his time, joker Shack paused before quipping: 'Ah yes, Walter, but what *side* of the net should I put it in?'

I later became a qualified coach and well remember the coaching jargon that Winterbottom himself coined. One such piece of gobbledygook went: 'On getting the ball use your peripheral vision.' What he meant was 'Watch your back!'

Norman Smith wagging his finger at joker Len Shackleton in a 1947 pep talk. From back left: Charlie Wayman, Ted Swinburne, Roy Bentley, Tom Pearson, Doug Wright, Charlie Crowe, Burke and Joe Harvey. Front: Norman Smith, George Stobbart, Len Shackleton, Doug Graham, Tot Smith and Frank Brennan.

The 1951 Wembley Cup Final will go down as the match that very nearly wasn't played. There was not one, but *three* crises, any one of which could have ended up with only one team on Wembley's red carpet to shake the hand of King George VI. Crisis number one loomed up in the shape of wise-cracking, briar-pipe-smoking, the late, lamented Len Shackleton. Wrote Milburn:

'That's why I came to admire Shack more than anybody. He insisted that we were playing for buttons. He insisted on this, way back to the war years. Aye! In fact, he came over just before the '51 Final – he was playing for Sunderland at the time – and spoke to the lads. "Hey, you want to refuse to go on the bloody pitch," he says, "because they're making nearly forty thousand pounds on the gate."

'It was three and a tanner for a ticket then, and about a couple of quid for a seat, or something. And Shack went through the whole routine of what they were clicking, the FA, and how much they were making, and what we were getting.'

Len Shackleton was a man before his time, not only with his inimitable style of play, but also his foresight into what was happening in the game at the time. A great deal of money was being made, with attendances holding up very well, although not as high as in the immediate post-war years. That the money wasn't going to us players was obvious, when the maximum wage at that time was only twelve pounds in season and ten in summer. Shack, together with players' champion Ernie Clay, was later to be instrumental in the FA taking a closer look at the whole idea of the maximum wage.

THE Jackie MILBURN ANGLE ON SOCCER

Made us feel like novices

THINKING of inside-lefts—as we must today in this series of mine — the first name which forces itself upon me is that of Len Shackleton, the "Clown Prince" himself.

Indeed, this always controversial character's name will always crop up whenever great inside forwards are talked about. For if ever there was a genius with a football it was Len.

Remember his amazing debut?

Tactics, plans, formations, etc., didn't mean very much to him for he played the game according to what he himself thought or felt at the time.

When Len Shackleton was "in the mood" he made the ball talk and, quite frankly, looking back, his ball control used to make his fellow professionals feel like absolute novices. Indeed, it sometimes gave us an inferiority complex!

Those lucky enough to be at St. James's Park when he made his debut for Newcastle United will never forget his display of artistry and his goal scoring ability when United beat Newport County 13—0.

It was a footballer's dream to play a game like that. For never could, or ever will, an inside-forward play a greater mid-field game and score six such brilliant goals into the bargain.

In the bath after the game a United player correctly summed it up when he said: "What the H— sort of player is this?"

"Shack" was, of course, something of a comedian both on and off the field, and one of the funniest incidents I ever remember occurred when we played at home to Cardiff City.

It was music-hall stuff

I scored a quick goal that day. I believe it was recorded as eight seconds, though Sandy Mutch, who had his watch in his hand, swears it was exactly six seconds.

However, we got well on top of Cardiff and "Shack" and Tommy Pearson started "antics" of ball skill and artistry the like of which I had never seen—real music hall stuff!

After a "mazy" Tommy Pearson dribble that brought the house down, he slipped the ball inside to "Shack" and then the fun really started.

Not to be outdone Len beat man after man within a ten-yard radius in a lightning dribble.

He had defenders lunging, jumping and throwing themselves at him but he just carried on in the one area with all of us just standing watching.

Soccer genius

LEN SHACKLETON — a genius with a football, says Jackie Milburn in discussing great inside-forwards.

Jackie Milburn admired Shack's skills, but he never rated him as a team player. That's why United sold him after less than two seasons.

The Newcastle lads decided not to take Shackleton's advice, however, the consensus being that if they refused to play, the board would soon draft in another eleven lads more than eager to pull on a black and white strip in a Cup Final. There was a saying: 'Shout down any pit shaft in the area and you'll get any amount of lads coming up good enough to play for Newcastle.'

Crisis number two was of a petticoat variety. Just before the squad left for Buxton, Ida Harvey, Joe's wife, noticed that the ticket she had been allocated for Wembley was a standing one on the terraces. On checking with my wife Ruth and other spouses it was found that, indeed, all the players' wives would have to stand. Ida, when roused, could be just as formidable an adversary as her husband, and she demanded that Joe, as skipper, should sort things out. No seat – no Wembley. Joe took another couple of players along for support when he approached Stan Seymour with the ultimatum. Seymour, sensing that with ladies involved this was one fight he couldn't win, said that the ticket allocation was an error, and the wives were given seats two rows behind the Royal Box. Yet another catastrophe had been averted.

Players' wives chat over a cup of tea. Included are: Mrs Norman Smith, Mrs Robledo, mother of George, and the wives of Brennan, Stokoe, Walker, Fairbrother, Cowell, Mitchell, Milburn, Crowe, Harvey and Taylor.

Not so easy was crisis number three. While at Buxton we had been give the run of the place and its facilities – snooker, golf, tennis, swimming, etc. – and everyone took full advantage of the very relaxed atmosphere. Even night-time drinking – in moderation – was allowed, but only up until the Wednesday night; after that a strict curfew was imposed, which players might defy at the risk of being sent home. Eleven o'clock was made the deadline.

Two players, Bob Cowell and Ernie Taylor, thought they could beat the system, and stayed out in Buxton until midnight. On entering the reception area, the pair spotted the four directors sitting in such a position that the errant duo could not fail to be spotted. Ernie decided he would try to enter the hotel through a window, while Bob, less adventurously, chose to sneak past the directors, still deep in conversation, by the more orthodox front door. Both were apprehended. Seymour demanded an explanation, and as the two unfortunates obviously didn't have one, they were told to wait in an adjoining room until it was decided what action would be taken. A few minutes later the miscreants were summoned before their betters and told they were to be punished, as had been threatened, by being sent home and their places in the team given to two of the travelling reserves.

The two lads were shattered. Totally shaken. Not for one moment had they suspected that the Boss would carry out his threat, but Seymour, backed up by his fellow directors, was adamant that a rule had been broken, and that those guilty of breaking rules must pay the penalty.

An uneasy Newcastle United party, players and directors, went to their beds that night not wanting to believe what had happened in the last couple of hours. Not just the two players, who saw everything they had worked for that season crumbling before their eyes, but also the management, because of the reception they knew they would get from a hostile press and an even more savage set of supporters should the errant pair – both crowd-pleasers – be dropped.

'If you have a problem, sleep on it' is a worthy old adage which worked wonders for United. Seymour awoke, accepted apologies from the two latecomers, and the good ship Magpie was back on an even keel.

Players relax outside the Palace Hotel, Buxton. From left: Cowell, Corbett, Crowe, Walker, Taylor, Stokoe, Mitchell, Brennan, Harvey, Robledo and Milburn.

The Newcastle squad left Buxton on the Friday morning to travel to Weybridge where we were to stay overnight at the Oatlands Park Hotel. The players' wives made their own way down to the capital the same day, having been booked into the Great Northern Hotel. Also in the Newcastle party were two Geordie entertainers who were to keep the players in high spirits the night before the game and also the morning of the match. At last we were relaxing and getting the 'feel' of the big occasion. We had climbed a mountain to get this far, but from now on it was all downhill.

After arriving at the hotel, unpacking, then having a light lunch, the players went with Seymour straight to Wembley Stadium, which was only a few miles away. The psychological advantage of a team walking on the Wembley turf a full day before they are due to take part in a big occasion like a Cup Final is tremendous. The players spent a full hour getting the feel of the dressing rooms, treading every bit of the lush turf, taking time to stand and stare without the attention of 100,000 pairs of prying eyes feeding off our every move, searching for cracks in our armour. And then it was the journey back – relaxing, joking, but with the mind's eye still keenly focused on the twin towers, shadowing that massive expanse of green.

The Saturday morning was spent pottering around the hotel grounds, playing snooker, table tennis, a friendly game of three-card-brag – anything to keep over-active minds from dwelling too long on the afternoon's affairs.

The two travelling Geordie minstrels, comedian Harry Goodfellow and his pianist Benny Needham, played and sang a medley of North Eastern favourites, including: 'She's a big lass and a bonnie lass ... And she likes her beer ... And they call her Cushie Butterfield ... And I wish she was here.'

After lunch it was time for George Robledo to leave for the game. George was a poor coach traveller, and Seymour, taking no chances, had arranged that Bobby Cowell and trainer Norman Smith should accompany the Chilean on the short train journey that would take them direct to the stadium. As Jackie Milburn waved them off, he shouted, 'I hope we see you later!' and when the full significance of that remark hit George, his face shadowed with a look of concern. 'You know, Jackie, I hadn't thought of that,' he said.

That's me with my eye on the ball, always a good rule at football or table tennis.

The coach containing the rest of the team arrived at the ground ninety minutes before kick-off; ample time to go through the superstitious rituals which footballers build up during a Cup run. Jack Fairbrother sensuously pulling on his policeman's gloves of the purest white; Bobby Cowell wearing a

Jackie and George always pulled their weight in United's attack.

particular tie; Frank Brennan with the battered boots, large enough to take little Ernie Taylor's size fours as the wee man climbed into them still wearing his own; Jackie Milburn with his ebony elephant, and captain Joe Harvey entrusted with a very special 1901 penny, already carried by two Newcastle United players in previous Cup Final victories, and now entrusted to Joe to carry to a hat-trick of wins. Dare he even think of failure?

Getting ready in the 'south' dressing room, some of the players were so worked up that they went into the toilets for a crafty drag. The sounds of *Abide with Me*, his favourite hymn, took Jackie, together with George Robledo – who had made it after all – down the tunnel to sneak a look at the singing crowd. They were there for only seconds before being beckoned back into the dressing room. A pity, for they missed the next song, conducted by Wembley regular Arthur Caiger, *Blaydon Races*. Strictly impartial, the band of the Coldstream Guards next struck up with *She's a Lassie from Lancashire*, satisfying both sets of happy supporters.

Now it was approaching ten minutes to three, and there began the long walk up the narrow tunnel, side by side and shoulder to shoulder with your opposition, afraid to glance across lest anxious eyes betray the fear which was turning sturdy legs to putty. Leading the parade of the gladiators was Mr John Whitty, a compact little man, bowler-hatted – marshal for the afternoon. A member of the FA, his job was to issue instructions to everyone so that they knew what was expected of them once out on the field.

On the pitch a game was already in progress: catch the duck! Blackpool hotelier Sid Bevers, dressed in a tangerine and white suit, had run on to the field carrying a large box which he placed on the centre spot next to the Coldstream Guards' band. Out of the box sprang Donald, a spotlessly-white duck that had been present at every Blackpool tie and was looked upon by the Blackpool supporters as unofficial mascot. Donald strutted and waddled for several minutes before the Wembley security police converged on him.

The Newcastle team for the Final was the familiar: Fairbrother, Cowell, Corbett, Harvey, Brennan, Crowe, Walker, Taylor, Milburn, Robledo and Mitchell.

NEWS CHRONICLE

COMMUNITY SINGING

Conducted by ARTHUR CAIGER, D.C.M.

accompanied by

THE BAND OF THE COLDSTREAM GUARDS

by permission of Col. E. R. HILL, D.S.O., Commanding Coldstream Guards.

Conducted by Capt. DOUGLAS A. POPE, A.R.C.M., p.s.m., Director of Music.

---

1 ABIDE WITH ME

Abide with me; fast falls the eventide;
The darkness deepens; Lord, with me abide!
When other helpers fail, and comforts flee,
Help of the helpless, O abide with me.

Swift to its close ebbs out Life's little day;
Earth's joys grow dim, its glories pass away;
Change and decay in all around I see;
O Thou Who changest not, abide with me.

Hold Thou Thy Cross before my closing eyes;
Shine through the gloom, and point me to the skies;
Heaven's morning breaks, and earth's vain shadows
　　flee;
In life, in death, O Lord, abide with me!

2 GOODNIGHT IRENE

Last Saturday night I got married,
Me and my wife settled down;
Now me and my wife are parted,
I'm gonna take another stroll down town.
　　　　　Chorus :
　　　Irene goodnight, Irene goodnight,
　　　Goodnight Irene, Goodnight Irene,
　　　I'll see you in my dreams.
Sometimes I live in the country,
Sometimes I live in the town;
Sometimes I have a great notion,
To jump into the river and drown.
　　　　　Chorus :
　　　Irene goodnight, etc.
(Reproduced by permission of Leeds Music Co. Ltd.)

3 LILLI MARLENE

Underneath the lantern by the barrack gate,
Darling I remember the way you used to wait
'Twas there that you whispered tenderly
That you lov'd me, you'd always be.
My Lilli of the lamplight,
My own Lilli Marlene.
Orders came for sailing somewhere over there,
All confined to barracks was more than I could bear
I knew you were waiting in the street,
I heard your feet, but could not meet
My Lilli of the lamplight,
My own Lilli Marlene.

4 BLAYDON RACES

Aa went to Blaydon Races, 'twas on the ninth of June
Eighteen hundred and sixty two on a summer's
　efternoon
Aa tyuk the bus fra Balmbra's and she was heavy laden,
Away we went alang Collingwood Street that's on the
　road to Blaydon.

　　　O' lads ye shud a' seen us gannin,
　　　Passin' the folks upon the road
　　　Just as they were stannin.
　　　Thor wis lots o' lads and lasses the wi' smilin're
　　　　faces
　　　Gannin alang the Scotswood Road to see the
　　　　Blaydon Races.

CHARLES BUCHAN former England, Sunderland and Arsenal Player
and well known Broadcaster

WILL REPORT ON THIS MATCH IN MONDAY'S

NEWS CHRONICLE

There was plenty of community singing at Wembley, as seen in this 1951 song sheet.

The duck, however, was enjoying the laughter and applause from the amused crowd, and managed to evade everyone until his owner, Sid, successfully captured the indignant bird with a rugby tackle.

And now we were emerging from the tunnel, Newcastle led by Stan Seymour, holder of one Cupwinner's medal, and Blackpool by Joe Smith, who had won two. The ripple of noise from those standing near the entrance turned into a torrent as we players came into full view of the 100,000 people who had paid a record of £39,336 to witness what had been hailed as the match of the century.

Introductions now, as a pale King George VI was guided towards the teams. He shook Joe Harvey's hand, asking, 'Have you played here before?'

'No,' replied Joe, 'but our chief has.'

Further down at the end of the Newcastle line, Stan Seymour confirmed, 'Yes, indeed. I had the honour of receiving a Cupwinner's medal from Your Majesty in 1924.' Formalities over, the two teams ran to their respective ends, looking up into the vast crowd trying to pinpoint friends and relatives bobbing around in that vast sea of faces.

It was a frail King George VI that greeted Newcastle United in the 1951 FA Cup Final at Wembley. There is a look of warm affection in skipper Joe Harvey's eyes as he introduces his Monarch to his best friend, Jackie Milburn.

The Blackpool side was: Farm, Shimwell, Garrett, Johnston, Hayward, Kelly, Matthews, Mudie, Mortenson, W.J. Slater and Perry. Blackpool had been forced to play an amateur, Bill Slater – who had not played in a First Division game for six months – because of an injury to their regular inside-left, Alan Brown. We fielded the side that had been promised our places after the semi-final, in spite of injury scares with Brennan and Harvey.

Immediately before the kick-off there was still a brisk market of tickets at Wembley Park Underground station. One young Newcastle United supporter openly touted a three-shilling ticket for four pounds, eventually having to be satisfied with three pounds ten shillings.

Referee Bill Ling got the game away at precisely 3 pm. Initial play was scrappy as both teams displayed obvious tension. But we were a confident, happy team and felt certain of winning. Milburn had the ball in the Blackpool net after ten minutes, chesting it down before sliding it past Farm. Ling thought that Jackie had handled the ball, and disallowed the goal. Jackie, on the point of protesting, remembered Seymour's last warning before going on to the pitch: 'On no account are you to question the referee's decisions.' He turned away, masking his frustration beneath lowered eyes.

Now it was Blackpool's turn to be disappointed. Matthews, target for all of the Seasiders' passes, evaded three tackles from Newcastle defenders before pinpointing the unmarked Slater. The unhappy amateur, with far more time than he realised, hooked his hurried first-time shot inches the wrong side of the post. Two relieved Geordies, myself and Bob Corbett, looked sheepishly at each other, having forgotten our original plan: leave Matthews to the nearest man, and don't get drawn out of position. The dejected Slater was probably unaware that he was only the third amateur to play in a Cup Final or, even more ominous, that both his predecessors had finished up on the losing sides. Meanwhile, the two Blackpool full-backs were also playing to orders. The policy of Eddie Shimwell and Tommy Garrett playing so far up the field and so dangerously square was not deliberately to set an offside trap, but to keep close to wingers Walker and Mitchell. The main reason for this was that Mitchell had had such a good game against Shimwell in the Cup rehearsal at Bloomfield Road only weeks earlier. The ploy worked in that they succeeded in keeping the wingmen quiet, but it left centre-half Hayward completely uncovered in the event of a swift counter-attack from the speedy Milburn. Purposely or not, the Blackpool defence caught United's forwards offside *nine* times in the first half. Most of the decisions were hairline ones, giving the impression that it needed the defenders to be only a fraction too far forward to let Newcastle in with a chance of springing the trap.

It was proving to be a dour, hard match, and from a Robledo tackle Blackpool captain Harry Johnston fell, writhing in agony for several minutes

Jack Fairbrother makes a complete nonsense of an attempted catch from a Perry corner, and was left marooned as Mortenson got a free header. The ball had 'Goal' embossed into the leather until ex-pit joiner Bobby Cowell miraculously emerged, as if from out of the Wembley turf itself, to head it off the goal-line.

before resuming with a definite hobble. At last Milburn showed his heels to the Blackpool defence after good work from Brennan and Taylor. Once in the clear he let fly from twenty yards, only to see Farm parry the ball with one hand, upwards and over the crossbar.

The half-time whistle went with Blackpool still looking like being the team to have a bet on. Fairbrother had taken thirteen goal kicks to five from Farm, and Blackpool had won three corner kicks to two from Newcastle. Half-time talk in our Newcastle dressing room was to the effect that it was 'so far, so good', with the proviso that more long balls, hit to the wings, might unsettle the opposing defence.

Newcastle chairman John Lee, sitting between Queen Elizabeth and the Duke of Gloucester during the first half, said later: 'I found Her Majesty enjoyed the football very much. At two or three stages she passed comments concerning offside and other decisions which showed me that she has seen quite a deal of football, and has followed it with enthusiastic interest.'

The game restarted at approximately 4 pm. The sun was in Fairbrother's eyes, and he donned a cloth cap.

Five minutes and twelve seconds later, Newcastle took the lead. Robledo came out of a tackle with the ball, looked up, saw his number-nine in acres of space, slotted the ball through to him, and stood back and enjoyed the lethal finish.

FA want to ban cloth cap at Cup Final

The FA had wanted Jack Fairbrother to wear a baseball cap as a cloth cap was supposedly too working class.

But the drama was far from being played out. Barely four minutes later, the Ashington man was centre stage once more to grab what many people have expressed to be one of the finest goals in a Cup Final. It sprang from a Blackpool error by, of all people, Matthews. Following the Newcastle opener, the desperate men in tangerine played every ball to the right wing in the hope that the maestro could save the game for them. But I hustled Stan Matthews, and he hurried an inside pass which went astray, and was then swept upfield to the Newcastle right-hand side. Ernie Taylor described what happened next:

'When I got the ball from Tommy Walker, I was wondering whether to try a shot or not, but out of the corner of my eye I saw a black and white shirt streaking along. I knew that only Milburn could move like that, so I decided on a back-heel.

'My back was to goal when I heard the thud of a shot, and as I spun round I saw the wonderful sight of the ball in the back of the net, and Milburn sitting on the ground grinning.'

Blackpool 'keeper George Farm is left stranded as Milburn (not in picture) scores the second goal.

The game had been won and lost in the space of five minutes. A crestfallen Blackpool side looked stunned as Mortenson got the game away again. But everyone knew that the spectacle was over, and that the Cup, thanks to two pieces of Milburn magic, was bound for Geordieland for the fourth time in their history; the luck of the 1901 penny lived on. Matthews did not star, thanks to Bob Corbett's good work, and I got my gold medal.

The remaining few minutes of the match were played out with the pathetic sight of Stanley Matthews, all hopes of a winner's medal gone for another year, trying to score a goal himself, so bereft of goal-scoring attempts were his colleagues.

But our jubilant Newcastle defence kept a firm hold on the game until referee Ling confirmed what everybody else had known for some time: it was Newcastle's Cup.

Even on Wearside, Sunderland

Fairbrother (in cloth cap) punches ball clear with Brennan, Cowell and Mortenson in attendance.

fans, fed up with watching their team playing out a dull 1-1 draw with West Brom, tuned in to a radio commentary of the Final and cheered like mad when Milburn scored his second goal.

Joe Harvey led us up the steps to receive the winners' medals, as a forlorn Blackpool eleven trooped off the pitch almost unnoticed. Both the King and Queen in presenting the Cup and medals thanked the Newcastle team for the entertainment they had provided. The Queen emphasised that she had thought the football very enjoyable. As a grinning Jack Fairbrother passed her, Princess Margaret remarked, 'A lovely day for you!'

After the medal ceremony it was back down to the pitch once more to acknowledge the 12,000 loyal fans who had played their own special part in the victory, spurring us with familiar chants and songs.

Joe Harvey, holding the Cup above his head, was lifted on to the broad shoulders of Frank Brennan and Jackie Milburn, with the rest of the laughing team grouped closely, making a fine tableau for the nation's press.

Back in the relative haven of the dressing room, the champagne corks popped and Jackie had his first taste of bubbly out of a Cup now bedecked with Black and White favours. 'By, that's champion!' said Jackie, licking his lips.

Now it was the turn of the reporters to get their own particular stories from each of the players. 'What about that second goal, Jack?'

Jackie smiled. 'It could have gone anywhere,' he replied modestly.

Statistically Blackpool would seem to have had more of the play, with Newcastle having to take twenty-six goal kicks to Blackpool's eleven, while Newcastle gave away fifteen free kicks against only two from the Blackpool side.

A losing Cup Finalists' dressing room is never a happy one, but Blackpool had already tasted defeat only two years earlier, which made it an even more desolate place. Manager Joe Smith was reported as saying that he thought the first goal had been offside. Asked about the second, he replied, 'I couldn't see it for a pillar.'

Stanley Matthews paid tribute to Milburn's two goals in an article some years later:

'It was definitely Milburn's match! His terrific speed made the first. He raced through a gap as wide as the Sahara desert to take a George Robledo pass,

Fans crammed Piccadilly, Leicester Square and Trafalgar Square where they sang Blaydon Races and the praises of the whole team. Not even a sudden downpour could dampen their joyous enthusiasm, and the festivities went on late into the night.

calmly drew George Farm, and slipped the ball into the net.

'The second was right out of this world! It was the greatest goal I have ever seen, and certainly the finest ever scored at Wembley. A goal that every player dreams about.

'That goal is now history, but how many other players would have chanced such a shot, especially in a Wembley Final? Very few would have had the courage. Certainly only a player with the Milburn brand of confidence in his own shooting power.'

After the game, a coach whisked us back to the Great Northern Hotel to enable us to change into best bib and tucker, for that evening we were off to a celebration dinner at the plush Savoy Hotel in London's trendy West End. Prior to that, however, the players met up with their wives, me with Ruth, Bob Cowell with Elsie, Jackie with Laura, and big Frank Brennan with Ethna, who offered kisses in return for a first look at the precious gold medal in the small blue box.

There followed a small reception when the players and their wives were joined by the directors to toast the team's victory in champagne. On the way to the Savoy, the Newcastle coach passed through streets bulging with jubilant Geordies intent on letting the world know who had won the Cup.

Over two hundred people were gathered under the brightly-lit chandeliers of the Savoy, and it is doubtful whether I knew a quarter of them. Faces I might have been expected to recognise were of members of Newcastle's great 1910 Cup-winning side: Peter McWilliam, Jimmy Howie and Jackie Rutherford. They were joined later by the legendary Bill McCracken, who hadn't even bothered to go to Wembley; he'd gone on a scouting mission for the club. 'I'd rather watch the on-coming youngsters,' he said. Of Jackie Milburn, Jackie Rutherford was quoted as saying: 'Here is one whom we would have been proud to have in the sides of my day.'

The previous three times that Newcastle had won the Cup had been in 1910, when they beat Barnsley 2-0; in 1924 when they again won 2-0, this time against Aston Villa; and in 1932 when Arsenal were beaten 2-1. In their four losing Finals, United had been beaten 2-0 by Aston Villa in 1905; 1-0 by Everton in 1906; 3-1 by Wolves in 1908; and 1-0 by Bradford City in 1911.

Back at Trafalgar Square, as darkness set in, some sympathetic North Eastern souls thought that Nelson looked a little cold and began to collect material to light a bonfire. Five London bobbies soon put a damper on that idea. Over in Piccadilly, reinforcement police had to be called in to keep the crowds moving, as large traffic jams were being caused by masses of Geordies who would suddenly stop and give a rendition of *Blaydon Races*.

Away from the genial mayhem, polite speeches were being made at the Savoy. Joe Harvey again praised his team; Arthur Drewry, vice-president of the Football Association, paid tribute to Stan Seymour and trainer Norman Smith, while at the same time hinting that the England selectors had taken note of 'some fine Newcastle United performances' – a clear indication that Milburn was once again in line for an England cap. The Duke of Northumberland, Viscount Allendale and the mayor of Newcastle, Alderman Chapman, assured the players that all the North East would be very proud of their achievement.

Newcastle United had a League game at Wolverhampton on the following Wednesday, and we decided to stay on at London overnight then move camp to the Royal Albion Hotel at Brighton until mid-week.

So it was not until Thursday, 3rd May that the FA Cup arrived on Tyneside, to be welcomed by close on a quarter of a million raucous Geordie supporters. The train carrying the Newcastle team in a specially hired carriage was coupled to an engine bedecked in black and white, bearing the slogan:

'IT'S OURS AGAIN'

Mr & Mrs Milburn and Mr & Mrs Fairbrother enjoy the sunshine from their Brighton hotel balcony.

The usually drab Central Station was dressed to the number-nines as the train swept into the main platform. The fireman and driver left their posts momentarily to thrust Newcastle's colours aloft as the train came to a halt beside an enormous banner that proclaimed:

'WELCOME HYEM, CANNY LADS'

First to jump from the train was Joe Harvey, the Cup held for all to savour. Policemen linked arms to keep back the good-natured crowd which threatened to swamp the platform in a deluge of black and white flags and scarves. Nearly 600 Tyneside bobbies were on duty that fine May evening. Most of them lined the 'victory route' which took the open-roofed bus up Neville Street, past a bewildered Lord Grey, through to Blackett Street and on to Gallowgate.

An estimated 200,000 Tynesiders shouted and sang themselves hoarse on the pavement, while others, leaning from second and third-floor office and shop windows, showered the coach with a New York style tickertape welcome. Frank Brennan remembered: 'We were all amazed, you know. All these milling masses – we had never seen Newcastle like this.'

More was to come. Another 30,000 people were packed into St James' for a Central League game as the news was announced on the loudspeakers at 6.40 pm: 'The Cup is back in the North East.' Forty minutes later the coach, with a huge mass of bodies snaking along behind it, arrived to a new welcoming cheer.

The Cup had cost fifty pounds when bought in 1910, after being made by a Bradford firm. It was, in fact, the third FA Cup to be used in the competition, which has been in existence since 1871. The first, which played such a thrilling part in the history of English football, was stolen on the night of 11th September 1895 from the shop window of a Birmingham football manufacturer. Aston Villa, the holders, were fined £25 by the Football Association for lending it out.

When the cheers for Harvey had subsided, a chant of 'We want Jackie' surged around the ground, gradually increasing in volume until the ever-modest Ashington collier's son sidled up to the microphone, right arm tucked self-consciously into his grey jacket. It was a further three minutes before the crowd would let him speak. He finally silenced them with: 'Come on, let's get on with it. I'm getting nervous stannin' here.' The fans needed no encouragement to laugh at this typical Milburnism. He continued: 'This has been the proudest moment of our lives.' And he turned to me, Mitchell, Harvey & Co for support. 'Hasn't it lads?'

'I think we must've kidded you on these last few weeks. But we knew in wor hearts that we could win on Sa'day. Anyhow, we darena' come back withoot it! We won because we have the finest bunch of lads in the world, the finest skipper, and the best supporters. Thanks a lot.'

The team appeared into St James' headed by Joe Harvey, still clutching the precious trophy, with goalscorer Milburn and Charlie Crowe and all the lads.

WATCH OUT ARSENAL WE'RE HEADING YOUR WAY, 1951/52

As Newcastle United players in the 1950s, we were not actively encouraged to find work outside the game. However, it was acknowledged that football was a precarious occupation and that some form of alternative income would be needed when it was time for us pros to hang up our boots. In the early 1950s, I was employed as an agent for a building contractor; Frank Brennan went into the sportswear business; and Jackie Milburn, as well as sponsoring cereal products and having a fireplace shop in Ashington, was given a luxury coach (as seen above) in which he transported the team on short jaunts up to Seahouses. But it was a channel hop next for me and the lads as we headed into Europe during the close season of 1951.

Newcastle officials planned a short seven-day tour of Europe for the us during the summer of 1951. It was a happy-go-lucky trip which none of the players took all that seriously. I remember that one of the games was against Anderlecht, the Belgian League champions, at the Heysel Stadium. It was billed as an exhibition match, but rumours were flying that the Belgians were on to a huge bonus if they beat the English FA Cup holders. The Newcastle lads were on to the usual two pounds for a win.

Ernie Taylor, proving just as wily off the field as on, persuaded Joe Harvey to ask the Anderlecht captain, Mermans, to 'square' the game. The plan was that if they played an exciting game with an equal number of goals being scored by each team, then the Belgians' bonus could be shared by everyone. Mermans, who later became chairman of the Belgian FA, was of the opinion that his side could beat us *without* resorting to collusion, and refused to enter into any bargain with the opposition. His decision proved ill-advised and cost him a lot of money as we thrashed Anderlecht 5-1.

That was when I needed a passport for the first time.

In August 1951 Newcastle had a brand-new season to look forward to, with the first game an English/Scottish Cupwinner's match in Scotland against the might of Glasgow Celtic. True to form, the Newcastle board managed to alienate some players right from the kick-off. For the game against Celtic – a highly prestigious and lucrative one for the team – four players from the Cup-winning team were left out; myself, Ernie Taylor and Bob Corbett while Jack Fairbrother stepped down to give Ronnie Simpson a game in goals. Seymour said at the time that it was to give a first-team blooding to others. But we were very upset, and voiced our displeasure. Seymour refused to change the team.

Ernie Taylor, around whom most of United's attacks were built, banged in a transfer request almost immediately. The Newcastle board saw Taylor's action as a fit of petulance and, not prepared to bend to individual pressures, agreed to listen to offers. Joe Harvey, when he heard that there was a strong possibility that his wee friend would be leaving, pleaded with Seymour: 'Stan, for God's sake, don't give the little fella a transfer. Transfer me – anybody! But keep Ernie; he makes everybody play.' Blackpool manager Joe Smith, obviously impressed with the little man's performance against his beaten Cup Final team, snapped up the talented midfield schemer, and Ernie went to the Seasiders in the October for £25,000. The whole Newcastle team suffered from his departure.

The next of the disgruntled trio to go was Bobby Corbett. Corbett, who began his career as a left-winger with Throckley, was a carefree lad, playing the game as if he really enjoyed it. Early in the 1951/52 season when United were away to Bolton Wanderers, Corbett misplaced a pass and Joe Harvey jumped on him straight away with his typical barrack-room manner, calling him a 'stupid bastard'. Bobby, very uncharacteristically, squared up to Joe, and for a few seconds feelings ran very high at Burnden Park. But it was just like God-bless-you to Joe, and both players were soon shaking hands and getting on with the game, the incident forgotten. Not so with Seymour, and a month later Corbett was off over the Transporter Bridge to play for Middlesbrough.

And yours truly was sore at missing the opening game and having been replaced in the first team by George Robledo's brother, Ted. So I asked to be placed on the transfer list. Seymour rejected my request and refused to discuss the matter. I called to see Stan Seymour, sometimes two or three times a week. Seymour used to shake his head and say, 'Resign yourself to the fact, you are not leaving Newcastle. No! No!' There were times when he wouldn't look at me. He had a swivel chair and he would twirl around and face the wall rather than look at me while talking. He was convinced I had been 'nobbled', that another team had talked to me. I was in the Reserves at the time, captaining the team alongside Jack Fairbrother, who had been dropped for Ronnie Simpson.

Simpson had joined United a couple of months before the Cup Final against Blackpool. A Newcastle journalist told Fairbrother then that he wouldn't be in the first team for the coming season. Jack, always one to take things to heart, packed his bags and was on the platform at Newcastle Central waiting for a train when Joe Harvey arrived to persuade the goalkeeper: ' … don't be so silly, Jack, forget it, and come back with me.' Fairbrother returned and played his part in winning the Cup, but when the new season got under way, sure enough, Ronnie Simpson was wearing the first-eleven goalkeeper's jersey. Jack later moved on to be player/manager of Peterborough, then playing in the Midland League, while I, still niggling away, played most of the new season in the Reserves.

The complete Newcastle United squad for 1951/52.

Messing around with the team hadn't been good for morale. In the early days we even stayed together during the summer months playing cricket for charity. This game was played at the County Ground in Jesmond. From left: Harry Robson, a pro for Lancashire, Tot Smith, S.G. Marsh a Northumberland pro, Jack Milburn, Bob Mitchell, Tommy Thompson. S.W. Hunt, Northumberland pro, me, Tommy Walker and George Hannah.

This was a game at Benwell. From left: George Hannah, Ashington lad Neville Black, Reg Davies, Bob Stokoe and yours truly holding on to the wicket-keeper's job.

And so it was that Newcastle United, who had finished on such a high note at the end of the previous season with a set of players that Jackie Milburn said were priceless, started rebuilding their side. The inside-forward position vacated by Taylor was filled by Billy Foulkes, who joined United from Chester for a record fee for a player from the Third Division.

In the 1951/52 season, we got off to a good start, although Jackie missed a number of the early games through a pulled leg muscle. With Newcastle now playing only one striker up front, George Robledo's name was the one filling the score-sheet. In our first four home games we amassed twenty goals, with only three against. After a game with the Reserves in the Central League, Milburn was soon back in the first team, and he and Robledo renewed a partnership in a United forward line that was to score ninety-eight goals by the end of the season. Four times Newcastle knocked in six goals, and twice they recorded seven.

One of the sevens was against old London rivals Tottenham. This is how Bill Stephens of the *Sunday Pictorial* saw that match:

'You needn't rub your eyes or polish your specs because that Newcastle 7 – Tottenham 2 scoreline is all too true. This is the story of how Newcastle exacted a terrific revenge for their seven goals defeat at White Hart Lane last season. There was no mistake about it either, and the champions can have no alibis.

'The Arthur Rowe (manager) Tottenham machine just failed to work for once, and from the moment four minutes from the start, when Ted Ditchburn ought to have come out but didn't, and was well beaten by Mitchell, the Spurs were back-pedalling. They were forced into errors by the speed and precision of Newcastle's confident attack, and were completely outclassed and vanquished before the seventh goal whizzed past Ditchburn 13 minutes from the end.

'I thought it was over at the half-way stage because more mistakes by Ditchburn gave Newcastle three more goals from Walker 13 mins; Robledo 17 mins; and Mitchell 35 mins. The Spurs, always trying to play their normal game, were beaten but never ruffled. They fought back and scored through Bennett and Scarth. The revival lasted only half a minute as Robledo crashed in two more goals in 63 and 71 minutes, completing his hat-trick.'

Milburn challenges Spurs' Alf Ramsey and goalie Ditchburn.

By the time the FA Cup-ties came around, Newcastle were already being shouted as favourites to win both the Cup and the League. In the Third Round we were drawn at home to Aston Villa. United's old manager George Martin, now in charge of Villa, anticipating a result, arrived at St James' Park two days before the game with a briefcase full of replay tickets to be sold on the Sunday after the game if it ended in a draw. He was probably hoping that Newcastle's luck would run out, as no team had won the Cup in consecutive seasons since 1890. The Villa side now contained three ex-Newcastle forwards: Thompson, Dixon and Gibson. Alf McMichael and Ted Robledo, who had both played only one game in the run-up to the 1951 Cup win, were now regulars in the Newcastle side.

Jackie Milburn, who was beaten by George Robledo in the race to be the first Newcastle player since the war to score a hundred League goals, got as far as ninety-

Ted Robledo, a left-half, brother of George, joined Newcastle from Barnsley in 1949. Height 5ft 8ins, weight 11st 4lbs.

nine a week before the Cup-tie when he scored against Preston.

Among the favourites to win the Cup again, Newcastle nearly came down at the first hurdle. Before a stunned Geordie crowd of 56,860, Aston Villa led 2-0 before fifteen minutes had elapsed. Billy Foulkes, in Ernie Taylor's old position, reduced the lead after twenty minutes' play. Then Villa were blitzed by two quick goals from Bobby Mitchell. Right on time, George Robledo pinched another for us, to leave the Midland side wondering just what had hit them.

TWO MINUTES MAKE NEWCASTLE HISTORY

Newcastle 4, Aston Villa 2

HISTORY at Newcastle! With nine minutes to go Villa looked easy winners. With seven minutes to go they were a beaten side, swept to Cup oblivion by the most devastating two minutes St. James's Park has ever known.

How could it happen? Newcastle looked a hang dog side. Desperate, but not even fighting, and every few minutes Villa's forwards were threatening to make it a 3—1 win at least.

Then Ted Robledo sent a pass to Bobby Mitchell. He was twenty-five yards out but he loosed a terrific shot that beat Martin all ends up.

From the restart Newcastle went straight back. Foulkes to Mitchell and the ball was in, to put Newcastle in front. And they came again a third time, Milburn sending one for George Robledo to get the fourth.

Villa's ex-Newcastle inside trio set about their job with terrific energy and skill. They had Brennan, McMichael and Cowell desperately miskicking and misjudging their tackles, and were two goals to the good in fourteen minutes.

Inside left Dixon got them both, the first after five minutes from a Gibson pass, and the second a wonder shot taken on the run.

Astonishing that in these fourteen minutes Newcastle almost totally dominated the game. Their forwards, with Walker and Milburn outstanding, and George Robledo beating everybody to get in some amazing headers, were all over the Villa defence.

But near things are not goals. They did finally round off a Mitchell-George Robledo move with a goal by Foulkes, the scoring pass being one more Robledo header.

This goal, after twenty-one minutes, pulled Newcastle together. Yet before half-time those Villa inside men had got their second wind, and it was Simpson who had to make the miracle saves

EARLY BIRDS

GEORDIE (to Magpie): "Wad ye believe it, heor's th' forst bunch o' letters askin' for tickets for next yeor's Cup Final!"

It was a close thing as we came from behind to beat Aston Villa and move into the next round.

United fans breathed again as the team began their Wembley march.

Newcastle were next drawn away to Tottenham Hotspur, the League champions. Spurs manager Arthur Rowe said of the tie: 'There's only one thing wrong with Spurs versus Newcastle – it should have been at Wembley!' But we had nothing to fear from the London club, because of that 7-2 thrashing we had given them at the beginning of the season.

Playing at Turf Moor on 20th January, Jackie slammed in his hundredth goal, but still ended up on the losing side as Burnley beat the black and whites 2-1. A feature of the game was an incredible seventy-five yard run by Burnley centre-half Tom Cummings, culminating in what Milburn later described as 'The best goal I've ever seen.'

On 21st January 1952, the Victoria Club, known all over the world as the racing man's Stock Exchange, held a call-over on the FA Cup. This year was the first time they had done this in the ninety-two years of its existence. The odds were as follows:

11-2	Arsenal
15-2	Portsmouth
10-1	Tottenham Hotspur
10-1	Liverpool
11-1	Blackpool
14-1	Newcastle United
14-1	Wolverhampton Wanderers
16-1	Chelsea
16-1	West Bromwich Albion
16-1	Middlesbrough
25-1	Stoke City
33-1	Birmingham City
100-1	Others (which included Man Utd)

Newcastle announced the same side for the *tenth* consecutive week to take on a Charlton team that had lost their last three games. United, although doing well, near the top of the League, were still looking for the same stability which had brought them success the previous year. Jimmy Seed, Charlton's popular manager, arrived on Tyneside, joking, 'I don't suppose Jackie Milburn is off with a cold or something?' He was referring to the late goals which Jackie had scored against his team the previous season when United had won 3-2.

I enjoy a game of cards on the train with Robledo while Mitchell and McMichael do likewise.

Unfortunately for the Charlton side, Jackie was on top form, scoring twice, Newcastle won 6-0, and but for veteran Sam Bartram's inspired goalkeeping could easily have smashed that 13-0 record, so many chances did we create.

United were now travelling in style, and we set off to Brighton for a week's training, in our own special railway carriage. It was split into two compartments, one for directors and one for players. The food was always first class and served from a galley. But if United chairman Willie McKeag didn't agree with something on the menu there used to be ructions in the galley. On each journey the players were given a packet of 20 cigarettes.

Soon after arriving at the southern resort, the mayor of Brighton arranged for a sherry party to welcome the group. Interviewed in Brighton by a *Newcastle Journal* reporter, Stan Seymour, director/manager, said:

'We've come here to escape from ticket touts. They've worried the lives out of all of us. The football public up there in Newcastle are Cup-tie mad, and it has been proving an ordeal for players and officials. A second reason for the trip was to give the players a break. They had a stiff Christmas programme and now face both Cup and League matches, which puts an extra strain on them.'

We always used to play on Christmas Day and Boxing Day, and sometimes it would mean three matches over four days, on a Friday, Saturday and Monday. That was the time of year when the trainer tried to say your injuries weren't as bad as you felt they were. As a player, you knew if you got a knock in the first game it wouldn't do you any good to go three matches together – but they always wanted you to play on. I don't know what the supporters thought we were doing, but we received a letter from a fan that said: 'I thought you played very well considering all that Christmas Pudding inside you.'

This could be me and Ron Batty chasing Mannion's shadow on a snow-covered pitch.

The fixtures people tried to give us northern opposition over Christmas, such as Middlesbrough, Sunderland, Leeds or Sheffield Wednesday, and we often played the same team, back-to-back. I used to get sick and tired of playing against a team such as Middlesbrough over the holidays as they had Wilf Mannion, who was the golden boy in those days. That was another reason you wouldn't have a drink – you couldn't if you had to play against someone like Mannion twice in two days.

With regard to ticket touts, there was a couple of fellows who we used regularly to pass on tickets, but the widest boy by far was Chips Rose from Newcastle who was a promoter of a football pools firm in Ireland. Chips featured strongly in an incident in 1951 when we were playing Wolves in a semi-final replay at Huddersfield. Fifteen minutes before kick-off, I received a message that my father and brother Ken were outside the ground and couldn't get in. Norman Smith had a couple of tickets which he gave me, then wrapped an overcoat over me (I was stripped and ready), saying: 'Go to the gate, Charlie, give them the tickets and get back here, quick.' I rushed out, gave Dad and Ken the tickets, but as I tried to get back into the ground I was confronted by a burly doorman who refused to let me in. Chips Rose was standing nearby selling his tickets. He rushed over, all official-like, saying: 'Don't you know who this man is? He is Newcastle United's left-half. Now out of the way, my good man!' With that he escorted me through the door and into the corridor leading to the pitch, saying: 'All the best for the match, Charlie, and many thanks – I was wondering how I was going to get in – I've sold all my tickets!'

Back at Brighton we trained at a greyhound stadium owned by one of the Brighton directors, but found there were no facilities for showers, so mini-cabs were summoned to ferry the players to a nearby gymnasium. In our hotel we were fed on the best, including liberal helpings of oysters.

The game at White Hart Lane – given the all clear only hours before kick-off by referee W.H.E. Evans – was played in atrocious conditions with players having to plough through a sea of clarts up the middle and skate over bone-hard surfaces near the touchlines. Spurs tried to play it too close and suffered accordingly. Newcastle, swinging the ball about the park, went into the lead with goals scored by George Robledo and Mitchell. In the final minutes the Chilean, prone on the ground and surrounded by three white shirts managed to hook his second, and United's last, goal as we cracked our London cup hoodoo to win 3-0.

Jumping out of the bath after the game, a jubilant Bobby Mitchell obliged with the following ditty, written to the tune of a *A Gordon for Me.*

Six oysters a day, then play Spurs away,
The tasty wee oysters worked wonders today,
The Magpies were braw, supporters 'n' a',
But the wee Brighton oysters take pride of it a'.

Some quick reactions after a one-sided game were:

Arthur Rowe: 'It was not our day, and it's no disgrace to lose anywhere to such a display as Newcastle's.'

Alf Ramsey: 'The better team won, and good luck to United's back-to-Wembley bid.'

Joe Harvey: 'A big hand to management for our grand holiday, and to the trainers who tuned up the whole team to such form.'

Jackie Milburn: 'All the lads say they are going for the League points just as hard as for a Cup bonus.'

The Brighton oysters worked wonders for Bobby Mitchell.

Jackie was referring to United's slide down the League the previous season, caused by a sudden rush of Cup blood to the head. But Cup fever ran even higher a couple of days later as we were drawn away for yet another tie, this time at Swansea. United had played only one post-war game at the Vietch Field, and that had been during the 1946/47 season when a 2-1 win for the

Magpies had helped to push the Welsh side into the Third Division.

Swansea, whose small ground held only 28,000, allocated 6,610 tickets to the Geordie club who could have found takers for that paltry amount in the bar of one of Ashington's working men's clubs. Ticket demand at Swansea was so great that the General Post Office there ran out of half-crown postal orders. They sold 7,000 of that denomination in two days.

"Jackie" with gloves on

SNAPPED at St. James's Park today training for tomorrow's F.A. Cup-tie against Swansea Town is JACKIE MILBURN, Newcastle United's centre-forward.

Milburn pulled no punches on or off the field.

In spite of the claims of Harvey and Milburn about fighting for League points, we were very disappointing in our next outing, going down 3-0 at Molyneux where Wolves had their goalkeeper Bert Williams back in the side for the first time in three months. Swansea were showing no such reluctance to have a go, and beat Birmingham 4-0 to record their sixth consecutive win.

Local radio and *Sunday Times* reporter, Arthur Appleton, was a BBC radio producer at the time. He said:

'The BBC asked me to record the sound of a Newcastle goal being acclaimed by the crowd. I followed them from match to match and they never scored a goal; they were keeping themselves for Wembley. I told this to Jackie Milburn many years later, and he said: "Whey, man, Arthur, you should've told us – we would have scored one for you."

In Porthcawl, where the Newcastle team were staying, an injury scare arose over Bobby Mitchell who had sprained his back, but he managed to go with the rest of the team to the cinema on the Thursday night, and duly took his place in the line-up for the match. On the morning of the game, Newcastle were installed as 4 to 1 second favourites to lift the Cup, behind Arsenal whose odds had shortened to 7 to 2.

Swansea, fielding a Geordie centre-forward, Ronnie Turnbull, played a very physical game against Newcastle causing them many problems. Mitchell scored the only goal of the match in the forty-first minute, but only a desperate last-minute save from Simpson prevented the Welshmen from getting a well-earned equaliser.

Virtually every house in the North East was tuned in to the Light Programme the following Monday to hear who the lads had drawn in the Sixth Round. But the wooden marbles could not have been more unkind – Portsmouth away – and a great groan went up over the Tyne that could be heard almost as far south as Scotch Corner! The fans immediately got out their maps and rulers to see how far they would have to travel this time. Already they had spent long hours and good money in support of their team, and with a 674-mile round trip to the Hampshire coast in the offing, their travels took on a Marco Polo look:

> Round Four: Tottenham Hotspur – 542 miles
> Round Five: Swansea – 624 miles
> Round Six: Portsmouth – 674 miles

The Portsmouth-Newcastle game drew out every superlative from all those privileged to see it. It was the 'Cup-tie of the decade', said the man from the *Sunday People* He wrote:

'I shall remember this as the greatest final Wembley never saw. Thrills? It had them all – and to spare. Clever football? Tons of it. Mistakes? Yes, a few; excusable too. And towering above everything it had a Milburn hat-trick, all worked into a grandstand finish ... as the game finished with Newcastle leading 4-2 the whistle blew and the crowd broke on to the field. Milburn disappeared in a scrum of jubilant Geordies, and every Newcastle man was mobbed in turn. We are all a step nearer Cup history. Newcastle, I salute you ... if anyone deserves a two-year lease on the Cup in these modern times, you do.'

But the most imminent question for United fans was: 'Who do we play in the semi-final?' As a result of the draw, Newcastle were to play Blackburn Rovers at Hillsborough, with Arsenal playing Chelsea at White Hart Lane. The Geordie team now became the bookies' favourite. The odds were: 6-4 Newcastle, 2-1 Arsenal, 5-1 Chelsea, 15-2 Blackburn. Tickets for the Newcastle semi-final went on sale on Friday 21st March. British Railways put their allocation of 4,000 on sale at 6 pm, but by then 6,000 people were in a queue which stretched from the Central Station to Marlborough Crescent bus station. Altogether, BR turned down block bookings for 15,000 unlucky fans. Thirteen train-loads eventually made the trip to Sheffield.

On 29th March, semi-final day, Newcastle were being called the 'Cup Team of the Century'. From 1905 they had appeared in *eight* Finals and had twice been beaten semi-finalists. Seven of the team who had Cupwinners' medals were there from the previous April. Newcomers were: the boyish looking Scot Ronnie Simpson, Ireland's new captain Alf McMichael, the younger Robledo brother, Ted, and Billy Foulkes, who since joining United had been capped by Wales.

Once again, Newcastle were held to a draw at Hillsborough in a semi-final match. Blackburn, far from being overawed by the Magpies' mighty

THE DAILY MIRROR   Monday, March 10, 1952

WHEN SPORT PAYS OFF TO THE NATION

By TOM PHILLIPS

THEY can sneer that sport is something for muddied oafs, flannelled fools, and clowns in comic costumes dancing around, whirling rattles until you are deafened. And clever people ask, "What is the use of it all?"

They will also tell you that bread and circuses were the downfall of the Roman Empire.

What fools they are! For the pattern of history can never be repeated.

If the thesis of historians is true, that the love of sport is the sign of a decadent nation, they will be damned by the beliefs of one Mr. Jim Bowman, director of the Northumberland and Cumberland division of the National Coal Board.

Mr. Bowman says this: "EVERY TIME NEWCASTLE UNITED WIN A CUP-TIE, EVERY MINER IN THE NORTH-EAST KNOCKS OUT AN EXTRA TUB OF COAL A SHIFT."

So it is that the inspiration of Newcastle's magnificent 4—2 victory over Portsmouth has sent these tough, bluff, good-natured Geordies hurrying back to the coal face to hew out the precious mineral which means so much to this country's economic survival.

What a pity the supporters of every one of the ninety-two League clubs are not like them. All our production problems would then be solved, the dollar gap could be bridged and the "cold war" sizzled.

So much for the power of Newcastle.

Portsmouth is a great club. We were astounded to find on Saturday after the match the players of both teams drinking a light beer or a ginger ale in the boardroom.

Normally in any club the boardroom is the holy of holies, where only directors and their close friends may enter, while in the true tradition of the feudal system players are kept below stairs in the dressing room or outside in the coach.

Pompey, having been put out of the Cup,

will, we hope, go on to win the League championship, they deserve to.

Two of Portsmouth's finest directors, Mr. Vernon Stokes and Mr. Harry Wain, will tell you that every man who has played for Pompey never wants to leave the club; and if he does he always wants to return. Could any club have a better Certificate of Merit?

Where else will you find players in a boardroom after matches being allowed to talk freely on the games? On Saturday, there was Jackie Milburn, Newcastle's centre forward and hero of the triumph, telling Jack Froggatt, the Pompey centre half, how he tricked him when he scored his third goal, which sealed the fate of the tie.

The greatness of Newcastle is the enthusiasm their dynamic play engenders among their supporters. The greatness of Pompey is their human approach to the game.

If we could only weld these two together in any game we would crush all-comers, anywhere, anyhow, any time.

'Every time Newcastle United win a cup tie, every miner in the North East knocks out an extra tub of coal a shift.'

51

record, earned the right to be treated as equals in their first gale-swept meeting. A goalless draw was probably more than a lethargic Newcastle United deserved. The game, and most of United's 20,000 travelling fans, moved on to Elland Road, Leeds, the following Wednesday.

This time Newcastle began with far more urgency, but squandered at least three good chances in the first half. Soon after the restart, Milburn got clear on the right wing and crossed to George Robledo who headed Newcastle into the lead, but with only ten minutes left, a young Ronnie Clayton supplied an accurate ball to Eddie Quigley who equalised for the Rovers. Then, with less than five minutes to go, a Robledo effort was handled inside the penalty area. All black and white eyes turned in the direction of Jackie Milburn, the team's regular penalty taker. Jackie lowered his eyes and walked away from the ball. Harvey chased after him. 'What the bloody hell is wrong with you, man?' Jackie rubbed his knee, indicating that he was carrying an injury. He was reluctant to take such an important kick, which would either take the team to Wembley for a second time, or perhaps knock the stuffing out of the whole team if he missed. Harvey swung around and looked about him; the Newcastle team turned away to escape his searching eyes. Losing patience, the man with the magic left boot, Bobby Mitchell, without being asked, stepped forward and hit the ball as hard as he could. It could have only been a couple of feet from goalkeeper Elvy's right ear, but speed and power of the shot left him rooted to his goal-line. Newcastle were a goal up, and back at Wembley.

Jackie Milburn always said that he had an inferiority complex because of being a Geordie, especially when we went to London which was United's jinx city even then.

With Arsenal also through, the Gunner's manager Tom Whittaker had this to say: 'It should be a crackerjack Final. Both teams have been to Wembley since the war, so the players know the ground and should have no Wembley nerves.'

While all this had been going on I was captaining Newcastle United Reserves towards their first title in the Central League. We had a team made up of many first-team players, and won practically every game, playing to huge crowds of supporters.

It was Chilean Ted Robledo who had taken my number 6 shirt and it was obvious from the way he was playing that he would take some shifting. So I went back to Seymour to ask when he would be prepared to let me go. Seymour made me a proposition, saying: 'Look Charlie, forget all this talk about wanting away and I might make it worth your while. What would you say if I offered you 100 Cup Final tickets?' Well, I was shocked, as up till then the reserve players had only been allotted 32 tickets. But there was more. Seymour continued: 'As well as that, I shall put your name down as a 'definite' for our forthcoming tour of South Africa.'

I knew a bargain when I heard it, so I agreed, and shortly afterwards the party to go on tour was announced. It was to be the Cup Final team plus Ron Batty, George Hannah, Bob Stokoe and yours truly, Charlie Crowe.

You see, Newcastle had arranged a mammoth ten-week close-season tour of South Africa, and letters were already winging in from Geordie ex-pats enquiring if the Magpies would be visiting their particular area.

On 9th April 1952, Newcastle, Sunderland and Middlesbrough were among nine First Division clubs who were fined fifty guineas for contravention of a rule regarding giving 'spending money' to players. It all resulted from a questionnaire circulated to all clubs in the Football League

Stan Seymour was United's manager in everything but name.

asking whether spending money was paid to players. Some replied with a No, others with a Yes. All those who replied in the affirmative, including Liverpool, were fined accordingly. The directors at Newcastle had been in the habit of giving us players two pounds a day 'pocket money' while away from home for more than a couple of days. FA regulations stated that one pound was the maximum, so the United board fell into line with this ruling, giving us players the statutory one pound ... plus a packet of Players cigarettes!

Newcastle continued to lose points in the League, prompting letters of complaint to the local press, including this comment from 'Frustrated Season Ticket Holder':

'Both last season and this, United had a remarkable chance of doing the Double. But what has happened? We all saw this last year: no win between semi and final. And this season: 6 points out of 18 since the Cup run started. We sit and suffer while Arsenal go out for every point.'

Arsenal had then gone seventeen games without defeat, and were only two points behind League leaders, Manchester United.

The following week, Newcastle went down to London for what was to be a Cup rehearsal game at Highbury. Obviously not wanting to show our strong suit, Seymour chose the following: Simpson, Cowell, Batty, Harvey, Stokoe, T. Robledo, Walker, Davies, Keeble, Hannah and Ashington youngster, Ken Prior.

Arsenal brought back thirty-nine-year-old

F.A. CUP—Sixth Round

Blackburn (1)..3   **Burnley** .. (1)..1
Nightingale,   Chew
Holmes, Glover
Att., 53,000.   Rec., £8,443.
Luton .... (1)..2   **Arsenal** .. (0)..3
Moore, Mit-   Cox 2, Milton
chell (pen.)
Att., 28,433   Rec., £6,159
Portsmo'th (1)..2   **Newcastle** (1).. 4
Gaillard, Reid   Milburn 3, Robledo
Att., 44,699   Rec., £3,611
Sheff. U. .. (0) .0   **Chelsea** .. (1)..1
  Bentley
Att., 43,677   Rec., £4,540

DIVISION 1

A. Villa .. (0).. 0   **Spurs** .... (0)..3
  Duquemin 2,
  Walters
Blackpool (1)..4   **Fulham** .. (0)..2
Taylor (E.),   Hill, Mitten
Mortensen 3
Derby .... (2)..4   **Preston** .. (0)..3
Neilson, Morris   Foster, Morrisen,
(pen.), Lee,   Finney
Harrison
Huddersf'd (0)..0   **Bolton** .... (1).. 2
  Lofthouse, Moir
Liverpool . (0)..1   **Mid'lesbro'** (0)..1
Jones (N.)   Mannion
Sunderla'd (1)..1   **Man. Utd.** (0)..2
Ford (pen.)   Rowley, Cockburn
Wolves .... (2)..3   **Stoke** .... (0)..0
Mullen, Hancocks 2

	P.	W.	D.	L.	W.	D.	L.	F.	A.	Pts
			Home			**Away**		**Goals**		
Man. Utd. ..	33	10	3	3	8	6	3	69	43	45
Arsenal	32	9	6	1	8	2	6	63	45	42
Spurs	34	12	1	4	5	7	4	63	47	40
Portsmouth	32	10	2	4	7	5	5	55	44	40
Newcastle ..	31	10	3	2	5	4	7	81	52	37
Bolton	33	8	6	3	6	3	7	52	51	37
Wolves	33	8	4	5	4	8	4	67	52	36
Preston	34	7	3	6	6	6	6	61	48	35
A. Villa	33	9	3	5	5	4	7	56	55	35
Charlton ..	33	10	3	3	4	4	9	57	56	35
Blackpool	33	10	3	4	4	4	8	52	52	35
Man. City ..	32	7	4	5	5	6	5	50	45	34
Liverpool ..	33	4	10	3	5	6	5	44	44	34
Burnley ...	32	8	5	3	4	4	8	48	43	33
Sunderland	33	6	4	7	5	4	7	54	53	30
Derby	33	8	3	5	4	3	10	54	65	30
Chelsea	31	7	2	7	4	3	8	41	51	27
West Brom	31	5	7	4	3	3	9	53	63	26
Stoke	33	5	5	6	4	1	12	37	71	24
Middlesbro' ..	31	7	3	5	2	2	12	44	73	23
Fulham	33	3	6	7	3	2	12	48	65	20
Huddersfield	33	6	2	9	0	4	12	38	69	18

With games in hand, we had been well placed to do the Double.

Leslie Compton at centre-half in place of Ray Daniel who had fractured his arm in a previous game. Seymour said: 'If Daniel is fit and chosen to play at Wembley, we could not possibly consent to him wearing a plaster in the Final.'

From our League encounter at Highbury, Newcastle brought back a point and a boxful of Cup Final tickets which some members of the Arsenal team had been unable to sell. Writing in the *Newcastle Journal* a couple of weeks before the big Wembley game, Stan Seymour was in a philosophical mood:

'In football today there are far too many men holding a seat and directors who do little or nothing to aid the game. There is a little army of people in the game for no more than a good time or to satisfy a personal vanity. I blame the system that operates whereby a few men holding block shares can control Club elections by use of the proxy vote.'

Here Seymour was taking a swipe at Alderman Willie McKeag whose family headed Newcastle's board until Sir John Hall took the reins and rocketed United into the Premier League.

Chancing their luck, Newcastle applied to the FA for permission to take the FA Cup with them to South Africa, depending, of course, on whether we were successful in our attempt to win it for the second time in a row. (Rather like Man Utd this year, 2001, booking into a Cardiff hotel near the Millennium Stadium because they thought that winning the Cup was a formality.) Our last League match before the Final was against Aston Villa and ended up with us thrashing them 6-1. It was a remarkable game for my pal, big Frank Brennan. It all came about because of what Hughie Gallacher had written in the *South Shields Gazette*.

Not many centre-forwards got past big Frank – even if they did wear Arsenal colours.

The offending article appeared under the heading: 'Hughie Gallacher's Soccer Round Up'. Hughie wrote:

'Joe Harvey is one of the most popular leaders Newcastle have ever had, and perhaps we have not long to wait to see Harvey in an administrative position at St James' Park. I think he would make a great success of it. If Frank Brennan could be a bit more *constructive* he would walk into Scotland's team. He can subdue the best of centre-forwards, he can trap a ball, come out of a tackle with it, but he does not always place his final pass to advantage.'

Now let Frank tell the Hughie Gallacher story:

'Hughie used to write a weekly football column for a local paper, and one day he'd written to the effect that I was just a 'stopper' centre-half. I said: "Right, Mr bloody Gallacher, I'll show you who's just a stopper!" The first chance I got, I raced out of my own penalty area with the ball and passed to Jackie Milburn, shouting, "Hold it." Jackie hared off up the right wing with the ball, and I bounded up the middle of the park. When Milburn got level with their eighteen-yard-box, I shouted, "Right, Jackie, now." Jackie placed it lovely for me to run on to and bang it into the back of the net. As I was running back to the centre-circle, I looked up into the stands and shouted, "That bugger's for you, Hughie!"

We finished the season in a modest eighth place, but set a new record goal tally of ninety-eight. For the first time in five seasons, Jackie Milburn was *not* the top scorer; this honour went to Chilean George Robledo with thirty-three goals, still short of Hughie Gallacher's own record of thirty-six goals in the 1926/27

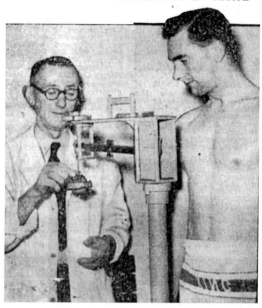

A fit Milburn added lots of weight to United's attack.

Brennan and I enjoy each other's company in the 1990s. Bet your boots that Frank would have scoffed that whole flan before he left the table.

season, and even further behind Albert Stubbins' phenomenal forty-four in thirty games during 1943/44.

I met up again with Albert Stubbins, on left, to wish good luck to Bobby Robson, Newcastle's new manager in the year 1999.

After that game, United again went down to Brighton to stay at the Royal Albion Hotel, but Joe Harvey stayed behind for treatment to an injury. The planned leisure itinerary for the week prior to the Cup Final Saturday was: Monday and Tuesday free; Wednesday golf at Roehampton; Thursday see ice hockey match; Friday go to the theatre.

An eleventh-hour move by Peter Dimmock, Head of Outside Broadcasting for the BBC, to broadcast the Final live on television was blocked by the Football Association. He remained optimistic, saying: 'We are still hoping the FA will change their mind. Since their last refusal to allow live broadcasts we have made several suggestions for a compromise.'

Back in Newcastle, British Railways said that 10,000 fans would be travelling by rail, 2,000 in dining cars. Over a hundred fans applied to travel by air, but lack of capacity limited this to only forty-three. Newcastle's most unlucky director was Dr Bob Rutherford; due to illness, this was the *second* Final he would miss.

With only two days left before the big day, a man walked into a Jarrow pub with a fifteen-shilling ticket which he said he would swap for a set of second-hand football strips for a team he ran. With no takers, he left mumbling something about having the precious ticket left on his hands. On the Friday night, seventeen train-loads of fans left the North East, the first departing at 10.40 pm from Newbiggin and Ashington.

Earlier that afternoon, the General Purposes Committee of the Football Association had stated that their previous decision *not* to allow the game to be televised would not be rescinded, and that therefore there would be no television coverage of the Final. They added that a telefilm would be shown on the Monday.

FACING THE FINAL
By Eric Thompson

THE five Newcastle United forwards complete this portrait gallery of a team facing their second successive Cup final. Their characteristics, ranging through directness, guile, speed, and strength, emphasise the variety contained in Newcastle's Wembley blend. It is this variety, the spice of Tyneside life, which gives colour to a team who play (as they have been sketched) in black and white.

Billy Foulkes, inside right (below), began the season with Chester and has since been capped for Wales and chosen for Wembley. Yes, the go-ahead type.

George Robledo, inside left (below), can make goals, take them, and (by the look of his muscles) break them. Attack is his best defence.

Tommy Walker, outside right (above), has direct ideas which his speed helps him to put into practice. The opposition left winger is wise to follow similar ideas before Walker falls back to take the ball off his toes.

Jackie Milburn, centre forward (above), the most graceful runner in Soccer. Fast off the mark and on the target. The biggest danger of them all, with shooting

Bobby Mitchell, outside left (above), with the dancing footwork. A football artist of moods and magic, with a daintiness that can prove deadly.

Eric Thompson of the Daily Mail was an excellent illustrator and analyst. Above: He scrutinises United's attack against Arsenal. Below: Eric analyses Jackie Milburn's second goal in the 1951 Cup Final.

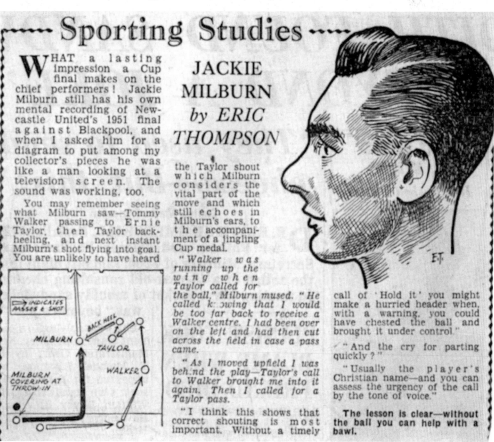

Sporting Studies

JACKIE MILBURN by ERIC THOMPSON

WHAT a lasting impression a Cup final makes on the chief performers! Jackie Milburn still has his own mental recording of Newcastle United's 1951 final against Blackpool, and when I asked him for a diagram to put among my collector's pieces he was like a man looking at a television screen. The sound was working, too.

You may remember seeing what Milburn saw—Tommy Walker passing to Ernie Taylor, then Taylor back-heeling, and next instant Milburn's shot flying into goal. You are unlikely to have heard the Taylor shout which Milburn considers the vital part of the move and which still echoes in Milburn's ears, to the accompaniment of a jingling Cup medal.

"Walker was running up the wing when Taylor called for the ball," Milburn mused. "He called knowing that I would be too far back to receive a Walker centre. I had been over on the left and had then cut across the field in case a pass came.

"As I moved upfield I was behind the play—Taylor's call to Walker brought me into it again. Then I called for a Taylor pass.

"I think this shows that correct shouting is most important. Without a timely call of 'Hold it' you might make a hurried header when, with a warning, you could have chested the ball and brought it under control."

"And the cry for parting quickly?"

"Usually the player's Christian name—and you can assess the urgency of the call by the tone of voice."

The lesson is clear—without the ball you can help with a bawl.

Newcastle supporters made a day of it in England's capital city.

Joe Harvey leads out a Newcastle United team back at Wembley for the second season in a row, unfortunately for me I had been replaced by Ted Robledo.

On paper there was little to choose between the two Cup Final teams as their skippers, Mercer and Harvey, two ex-Army sergeant-majors, swapped yarns on the centre circle with referee Arthur Ellis prior to the kick-off. Arsenal's line-up was: Swindon, Barnes, Smith, Forbes, Daniel, Mercer, Cox, Logie, Holton, Lishman and Roper. Newcastle fielded: Simpson, Cowell, McMichael, Harvey, Brennan, T. Robledo, Walker, Foulkes, Milburn, G. Robledo and Mitchell.

The official Wembley programmes in those days only cost one shilling, but then it could cost as little as three and a tanner to see the match itself.

Ronnie Simpson and Bob Cowell combine to clear their lines.

Simpson gathers with McMichael on the far post.

The game began quietly with neither attack threatening to crack open solid defences. Suddenly there was drama. Running for the ball with no-one near him, Arsenal full-back Wally Barnes turned sharply then keeled over, clutching his leg. It was a bad injury.

Here is the incident as described by Barnes in his book *Captain of Wales*.

'How does it feel, Wally?'

'Not so good.'

Billy Milne the Arsenal trainer sighed and shook his head, saying, 'Well, that's it, I'm afraid. Better make your mind up that you've had it this time.'

There was no doubt that trainer Billy Milne was right. That was the end of the 1952 Cup Final for me. Billy helped me off the field

Jackie Milburn looks on as his friend George Robledo scores the only goal of the game.

and into the dressing room, and the thought uppermost in my mind was that I had let the rest of the lads down. How could they possibly avoid defeat now, with only ten men and an hour to play?

'Later, as I lay on the table in the dressing room with Billy Milne to comfort me, messages from the field bolstered our hopes slightly. And when there were only seven minutes left to play, and still no score, we even started to think that the boys might achieve the impossible: hold out and force a replay. Then we heard a roar from the crowd, and Billy and I exchanged a glance. There was something awfully conclusive about that cheer.

'We heard slow, hesitant footsteps approaching down the tunnel and, after a pause, the door opened to reveal the figure of a very dejected-looking dressing-room attendant. He seemed at a loss for words to tell his news. At length he said: "We're one down." Quite unconsciously he had employed the personal pronoun "We". That dressing-room attendant must have seen dozens of Cup Finals and big international matches at Wembley. Great dramas were everyday events in his life. But obviously this match was affecting him like no other had done; all his emotion had become entangled in it, and there was no doubt on which side his sympathy lay.'

Jackie Milburn had this to say about the game:

'That May afternoon, Arsenal gave one of the greatest displays of courage I've ever experienced on a football field. From the moment Wally Barnes was injured until the end of the match, the Londoners kept themselves in the game. And I say this after making full allowance for the Newcastle United team playing really badly.

'There was even a lack of drama about the goal that won us the match. Mitchell put over a centre, and it seemed a lifetime as Robledo's header floated slowly through the air, hit an upright, and glided over the line. There was a tremendous roar of excitement from the Geordies in the crowd. Yet there was none of the tension ... and I for one did not feel the satisfaction of the previous year.'

Frank Brennan said almost the same thing: 'It was nothing like the first time. Nothing ever is. First time is always the best.'

Prime Minister Winston Churchill did the honours for Joe Harvey in 1952.

For a change, let the ladies have the last word.

Mrs Stan Seymour: 'It was very interesting to be in the Royal Box. I should have loved it for the Queen to be present, though Mr Winston Churchill was a great deputy.'

Mrs Ida Harvey: 'It was a terrible game. Arsenal played the football, and I was mightly glad when it was over.'

This time it is Frank Brennan and George Robledo who hoist their skipper on to their broad shoulders.

Mrs Ethna Brennan: 'It was a harassing game, but I thought we had the better chances.'

Mrs Laura Milburn: 'I was a bundle of nerves. I kept kneading my handkerchief and tearing the corners.'

Mrs Isobel Mitchell: 'I was eating a sweet and smoking a cigarette at the same time, as we waited for that goal which it seemed would never come.'

Mrs Elsie Robledo (George and Ted's mother): 'I wondered when George was going to get going.'

The *Sunday Express* correspondent summed up this dour match for everyone:

'This victory was a hollow as a kettledrum.'

The 100,000 spectators at Wembley paid over £44,000 to see the game. Newcastle players, by previous arrangement, were rewarded as follows:

Third Round	v Aston Villa	£2-0-0
Fourth Round	v Spurs	£4-0-0
Fifth Round	v Swansea	£6-0-0
Sixth Round	v Portsmouth	£8-0-0
Semi-final	v Blackburn	£7-10-0
Semi-final replay	v Blackburn	£15-0-0
Cup Final	v Arsenal	£20-0-0

Newcastle went into a holiday mood to welcome back their team with the precious trophy for a second time. Dare they think of a hat-trick of victories?

A celebration dinner was again held at the Savoy Hotel, and the Newcastle party stayed overnight at the Great Northern Hotel before coming home on the Monday. Their train was due in at 6.20 pm, and the whole area adjacent to Newcastle's Central Station stayed closed to traffic from five o'clock. The train stopped at Durham Station for Alderman McKeag to get off and dash the remaining dozen miles on his own. This ploy was to enable him to greet the players in his official capacity as Lord Mayor of Newcastle.

As the train pulled alongside the platform, there was a mini-Gallowgate roar from the 500 people the police had allowed into the station. The stone pillars were swathed in black and white, contrasting with the vivid crimson carpet laid out to welcome the team. The engine hissed to a stop beside a huge board which declared:

WELL DONE LADS
IT'S STILL WORS

On the side of the engine was another placard showing the years that Newcastle had won the Cup:

IT'S STILL WORS
1910-1924-1932-1951-1952

First off the train was Joe Harvey, Cup held high as in the previous year. He was greeted by Ald McKeag, now dressed in sable, and United's

POLICE ARE SWAMPED
IN RUSH OF CHEERING FANS

TYNESIDE MAKES A NIGHT OF IT

'om KENNETH MOOR   NEWCASTLE-ON-TYNE, Monday.

'R an hour tonight this was a city gone mad as 300,000 people swept aside barriers and police cordons to thunderous welcome to the Newcastle United team, ome from Wembley for the second successive year e Football Association Cup, which they retained Arsenal on Saturday.

Packed thousands outside the station roared as Joe Harvey, captain of the team, held the Cup aloft while the players climbed into an open-topped coach for the three-quarter-mile journey to the St. James's Park ground.

'New York' scene

Thousands more jammed the pavements, clung to lamp-posts, balanced on window-sills, and perched in trees.

From the tall buildings on either side waste paper and streamers cascaded in a New York-style welcome.

Twice the perspiring police trying to hold back the sea of people closing in behind the coach were overwhelmed and disappeared. Streets off the main route were solid with people craning their necks for a glimpse of the trophy.

Reinforced until their strength was 500, using a fleet of patrol cars and mounted officers, the police were swept away by the tide of delirious Tynesiders. Newcastle had never known anything like it.

George Robledo, whose goal brought the Cup to Newcastle for the fifth time, grinned at a poster: "Robledo for Lord Mayor."

It took the team 30 minutes to cover the three-quarters of a mile to St. James's Park, where 50,000

more people were waiting. With a band playing "Blaydon Races," the team paraded round their ground.

Alderman McKeag told the crowds: " I am proud to extend a civic welcome to this gallant team. Who knows—next year we might even make it a hat-trick."

When the storm of cheers had died away, deputy chairman Mr. Stan Seymour declared: " It's asking a lot, but we'll certainly have a try."

A chant of " We want George " brought Robledo to the microphone. He said: " Everyone in London and the South seems to be of the opinion that Arsenal should have had the Cup, but I am proud that we brought it back to Tyneside."

After the speeches there was a cake to cut—a 40lb., 2½ft.-long replica of Wembley Stadium.

Then the team went to their gymnasium to see a special newsreel of themselves equalling a 61-year-old record by winning Soccer's highest honour two years running.

Tonight the players and their wives joined the directors and club officials in a champagne celebration in the board-room at St. James's Park.

AT THE STATION.—The Lord Mayor of Newcastle, Alderman William McKeag, greets the Cup winners' captain, Joe Harvey, with a warm handshake when he officially welcomed the team on their arrival at Central Station last night.

Newcastle United's homecoming in 1952 was covered in every national daily newspaper.

official mascot, Peter Anderson of Byker, immaculate in a black and white striped suit, topper and bow tie. As reported in the *Newcastle Journal* the next day, McKeag made a short speech: 'You made me a proud man – next year we might make it a hat-trick.'

Then the procession set off through the streets of Neville, Collingwood, Grey and Blackett, before entering Gallowgate. The orderly, good-humoured crowd packed the pavements fifty deep all along the route. Millions of pieces of paper and confetti showered down on the players as the office girls once again gave their heroes a jamboree welcome. As the coach pulled into St James' a great roar went up from the 45,000 crowd who had waited patiently for over two hours.

A smiling Joe Harvey emerged with the Cup still in his hands. Behind him, limping slightly, was Jackie Milburn. Harvey, tired of holding the Cup, passed it on to Bobby Cowell, and grabbed the mascot's topper which he placed at a jaunty angle on his head. The fans loved that. After parading around the outside of the pitch, the players went up to the directors' box for the obligatory speeches. This time the chant from the women in the crowd was: 'We want George,' and the embarrassed 'Pancho' obliged, thanking them for their support.

Festivities in Newcastle went on until the small hours with thousands of people thronging the dancehalls and theatres. At the Grand Theatre in Byker, Tyneside's Little Waster, Bobby Thompson, amused his audience with a comic commentary on the match, while Yeoman's Sparkling Terriers reproduced the Final in canine fashion, properly attired in scarlet, and black and white.

Here are the final League tables

ENGLISH LEAGUE (Division I)

	P	W	D	L	F	A	W	D	L	F	A	Pts
Chels'a	42	11	5	5	43	39	9	7	5	34	28	52
Wolves	42	13	5	3	58	30	6	5	10	31	40	48
Prtsth	42	13	5	3	44	21	5	5	9	30	41	48
Sundld	42	8	11	2	39	27	7	7	7	25	27	48
Man U	42	12	4	5	44	30	8	3	10	40	44	47
Villa	42	11	3	7	58	31	9	4	8	34	42	47
Man O	42	11	5	5	45	36	7	5	9	31	33	46
Newcle	42	12	5	4	53	27	5	4	12	36	50	43
Arsenal	42	12	3	6	44	25	5	6	10	25	38	43
Burnly	42	11	3	7	29	19	6	6	9	22	29	43
Evertn	42	9	6	6	32	24	7	4	10	30	44	42
Hudsfd	42	10	4	7	28	21	4	9	8	35	45	41
Shef U	42	10	3	8	41	34	7	4	10	29	52	41
Prestn	42	8	5	8	47	33	8	3	10	36	31	40
Chrltn	42	8	6	7	43	34	7	4	10	33	41	40
Spurs	42	9	4	8	42	35	7	4	10	30	38	40
W.B.A.	42	11	5	5	44	33	5	3	13	32	63	40
Boltn	42	10	4	4	45	29	2	7	12	17	40	39
Black'l	42	8	6	7	33	26	6	4	11	27	38	38
Cardiff	42	9	4	8	41	38	4	7	10	31	38	37
Leics.	42	9	6	6	43	32	3	5	13	31	54	35
Shef W	42	7	7	7	42	38	1	3	17	21	62	26

ENGLISH LEAGUE (Division II)

	P	W	D	L	F	A	W	D	L	F	A	Pts
B'ham	42	14	4	3	56	22	8	6	7	36	25	54
Luton	42	12	4	5	55	18	5	6	10	33	35	54
Rothm	42	17	1	3	59	22	3	8	10	35	42	54
Leeds	42	13	4	4	43	19	9	3	9	27	34	53
Stoke	42	12	5	4	38	17	9	8	7	31	29	52
Bkbrn	42	14	4	3	73	31	8	2	11	41	48	50
Nots C	42	16	3	4	46	27	7	3	11	28	44	48
W Ham	42	12	4	5	46	28	6	6	9	28	42	46
Bris R	42	15	4	2	52	23	3	3	14	23	47	45
Swans	42	15	3	3	58	28	2	6	13	28	55	43
L'pool	42	11	7	3	55	37	5	3	13	37	59	42
Midbro	42	13	1	7	48	31	5	5	11	25	51	42
Bury	42	10	5	6	44	35	5	6	10	33	37	41
Fulhm	42	10	4	7	46	29	4	6	11	30	50	39
Nots F	42	8	4	9	29	29	4	3	10	29	33	39
Lincln	42	8	4	9	29	29	4	3	14	36	38	39
P Vale	42	10	6	5	31	21	2	5	14	17	50	35
Doncs	42	6	8	5	34	24	3	2	16	23	61	35
Hull	42	7	5	9	30	35	5	8	11	14	34	24
Plymth	42	10	4	7	29	26	2	3	16	28	56	31
Ipswh	42	10	3	8	37	28	1	3	17	20	64	28
Derby	42	8	6	9	39	34	1	3	17	16	48	23

ENGLISH LEAGUE (Div. III N)

	P	W	D	L	F	A	W	D	L	F	A	Pts
Brnsly	46	18	3	2	51	17	12	2	9	35	29	65
Accgtn	46	18	2	3	65	32	7	9	7	31	35	61
York	46	13	8	5	43	27	11	5	7	49	36	58
*Scunte	45	14	6	3	45	18	9	5	8	35	34	57
H'pools	45	16	3	4	39	20	9	2	12	25	29	55
C'field	45	17	1	5	54	33	7	5	11	27	37	54
G'head	45	11	5	5	38	26	9	5	9	27	43	52
Wrktn	45	11	7	5	39	23	7	7	9	29	32	50
Stckpt	46	13	4	6	50	27	5	8	10	34	43	48
Oldh'm	46	14	5	4	47	22	5	5	13	27	46	48
R'dale	45	13	7	3	39	20	4	7	12	30	46	48
*Sthpt	45	10	8	4	27	17	6	7	10	19	26	47
Mansfd	45	14	4	5	40	28	4	5	14	25	43	45
Halifx	45	9	5	9	41	28	6	4	13	22	40	43
Darlgn	45	10	7	6	41	28	4	7	12	21	45	42
Bradfd	46	11	7	5	29	21	4	4	15	27	49	41
Barrow	46	12	4	7	39	34	5	2	16	31	55	40
Wrexm	46	9	6	8	40	35	4	6	13	25	42	38
T'mere	46	9	6	8	37	30	4	5	14	18	40	37
Carl'le	46	12	1	10	53	39	3	5	15	25	50	36
Brad C	46	9	5	9	30	26	4	5	14	17	29	36
Crewe	46	8	10	5	45	35	2	4	17	23	56	34
Grimby	46	10	4	9	28	32	3	4	16	19	46	34
Chester	46	10	3	10	23	25	2	6	15	21	52	33
*Not including yesterday's result												

ENGLISH LEAGUE (Div. III S)

	P	W	D	L	F	A	W	D	L	F	A	Pts
Bris C	46	17	4	2	62	22	13	6	4	39	25	70
Leyton	46	16	2	5	48	20	10	7	6	41	27	61
Soton	46	16	6	1	49	19	8	5	10	26	32	59
Gill'm	45	12	8	3	41	28	8	7	8	36	38	55
Mill'all	45	14	6	3	44	25	6	5	12	28	43	51
Bri'ton	45	14	4	5	47	27	6	6	11	29	36	50
Watf'd	45	11	9	3	45	26	7	3	11	26	36	50
Torq'y	45	12	6	5	51	39	6	6	11	31	43	48
Cov-try	45	15	3	5	50	26	3	5	13	22	13	47
Sou'nd	45	13	5	5	48	28	4	7	12	35	52	46
Bren'd	46	11	6	6	44	36	5	8	10	38	46	46
Nor'ch	46	13	5	5	40	23	5	5	13	20	37	46
N'th'n	46	13	5	5	47	27	6	3	14	26	54	46
Alder't	45	12	6	5	44	23	4	7	12	31	48	45
Q.P.R.	46	13	7	3	46	25	2	7	14	23	50	44
S'bury	46	14	5	4	49	24	2	5	16	21	54	42
Read'g	46	7	10	6	32	26	6	5	12	31	47	41
Newp't	46	8	8	7	32	29	3	8	12	28	44	38
Palace	46	9	11	3	32	24	2	5	16	20	56	38
Swin'n	46	10	8	5	30	19	1	7	15	16	45	37
Exeter	46	9	7	7	30	31	2	8	13	17	42	37
Walsall	46	9	6	8	49	36	1	8	14	26	50	34
Col'ter	46	7	6	10	33	40	2	7	14	20	51	31

SCOTTISH LEAGUE (DIV. "A")

	P	W	D	L	F	A	W	D	L	F	A	Pts
Aber'n	30	14	0	1	41	9	10	1	4	32	17	49
Celtic	30	10	4	1	42	16	9	4	2	34	21	46
Rang's	30	13	2	0	40	8	6	1	8	27	25	41
Hearts	30	10	2	3	40	25	6	5	4	34	20	39
Hibs	30	8	5	2	52	23	7	2	6	36	31	34
S Mir	30	8	3	4	31	23	4	5	6	24	31	32
Clyde	30	6	7	2	33	20	5	2	8	26	30	31
D'ndee	30	9	2	4	32	21	4	2	9	16	27	30
Part'k	30	5	5	5	24	29	6	2	7	25	32	29
Kilm'k	30	5	3	7	18	24	5	3	7	28	34	26
E Fife	30	6	1	8	32	35	3	5	7	19	27	24
Falk'k	30	6	3	6	28	23	2	2	11	14	31	21
Q of S	30	7	2	6	22	29	2	4	9	16	27	24
Raith	30	8	2	5	31	25	1	3	14	23	42	23
Moth'l	30	8	2	5	42	23	1	4	10	18	39	24
Stirl'g	30	3	1	12	15	40	0	1	14	14	65	6

SCOTTISH LEAGUE (DIV. "B")

	P	W	D	L	F	A	W	D	L	F	A	Pts
Dnfmn	30	12	2	1	45	17	7	2	6	27	23	42
Afrdrie	30	13	2	0	62	26	5	3	8	41	35	40
Hamtn	30	10	3	2	38	20	7	2	6	36	31	39
Q Pk	30	7	4	4	33	15	8	1	6	32	21	35
Stnse	30	6	3	6	40	29	6	5	4	30	22	32
T Lan	30	10	1	4	41	20	3	6	6	22	29	33
S J'hn	30	8	1	6	31	21	7	1	7	23	30	32
Ayr U	30	10	3	2	36	20	4	1	10	25	53	32
Mortn	30	7	4	4	31	24	5	1	9	27	45	29
Forfar	30	7	3	5	35	31	4	3	8	28	42	28
Albn	30	5	5	5	34	34	3	5	7	16	35	26
Artth	30	5	4	5	28	28	2	4	9	27	44	24
Dun U	30	5	3	7	35	32	3	3	9	20	38	22
Cdbth	30	4	2	9	29	41	4	3	8	26	31	21
Alloa	30	3	6	6	29	31	4	0	11	22	44	20
Brchn	30	4	1	10	28	44	4	2	9	25	45	19

The League tables at the end of the 1951/52 season saw some familiar names in unfamiliar places in the tables.

Games between Newcastle United and Sunderland could be relied on to raise the temperature both on and off the pitch. This Roker Park goalmouth battle sees three Newcastle men: Hannah, Brennan and Cowell, seeing off Sunderland's England international, Willie Watson.

SECTION FOUR

THE LEAN YEARS AND IN-BETWEEN YEARS, 1952-1954

When Stan Seymour told me that I was to go on a tour of South Africa, I thought that it would be like going on holiday. In reality, we played 16 games in sizzling sunshine on rock-hard pitches. And as seen above, it was very much short-sleeve order as I challenged the goalkeeper at Durban.

On 11th May 1952, the first of the United party left for South Africa on the Pullman train 'Northumbrian'. So began a journey that was to take them 20,000 miles, of which 16,000 miles would be by air. For safety reasons the team travelled in two groups, the first being made up of directors Seymour and Taylor together with Harvey, Simpson, Cowell, Walker, Davies, Foulkes and Mitchell; they were to be joined in London by Ted Robledo, who had been spending a short holiday in the capital.

As the train pulled away from the Central Station platform, Joe Harvey waved and shouted, 'All the lads are looking forward to having a grand time over there, and we hope to do Newcastle credit.'

Stan Seymour qualified his captain's remarks: 'What we really want to do is show the South Africans what a grand game football is, and help them as much as possible in developing it.'

The second group, consisting of Lord Westwood, Norman Smith and players McMichael, Batty, Brennan, Milburn, G. Robledo, Hannah, Stokoe and myself, left two days later. Typically, when the train was due to leave, Frank Brennan still had not arrived. Seconds before departure Big Frank ambled up to join the rest of the group. An anxious Norman Smith enquired about Brennan's apparent lack of luggage. Funny man Frank pointed to his breast pocket, out of which peeked a toothbrush. 'I didna forget it, Norman; it's all there!'

United wonder tour can be rated a gamble

Newcastle United, Wembley winners of 1952, leave home today and tomorrow for London to embark on the biggest close season soccer tour of all time.

From London Airport they travel by air to Johannesburg to begin a tour that will entail an all in journey of over 20,000 miles including over 16,000 by plane to play 15 games against selected sides in South Africa.

NOT until July 20 will they set foot again in England. Within a week they will be recalled to report at St. James's Park to prepare themselves for the new League campaign. It is a wonder tour that is costing the sponsors, the South African Football Association, over £16,000.

The itinerary records a non-stop programme that allows for only two free days. It will be for the team—here today, there tomorrow—embracing at least two games in various parts of South Africa each week.

Life-time tour

THEY will be called on to make hops by air of over 1,000 miles to reach destinations and they will travel by rail jaunts that will keep them train bound for over 15 hours on single trips. Without doubt this close season trip is a travel opportunity of a lifetime for the "Magpies," but what will be the reaction, for without doubt the tour must be labelled as soccer's biggest gamble of season 1952-53.

Well might the mighty "Magpies" return to the next campaign leg weary, travel weary, and in need of the rest that the vast majority of other players have enjoyed.

Aftermath

Remember they go out as F.A. Cup winners to South Africa and with them goes the silver trophy for the first time out of Great Britain in history.

This South African tour might well prove to have a soccer aftermath that "Geordie" will regret.

The players, wherever they travel, are going to be lauded, feted, wined and dined. They are going to be invited here, there and everywhere to attend a round of parties and hero worshipped like no team has been before by the hosts that await their arrival.

The fact that they take with them the F.A. Cup will tend to aggravate the situation.

Last season Wolverhampton Wanderers made the tour, but they returned to stage a struggle to retain their reputation in the League battles that immediately followed their return.

And Wolves, it is a soccer certainty, were not the attraction the United, as Wembley winners, will be.

In many halts the team will find themselves in a humidity that will be near overpowering thousands of feet up, and in other towns they will be switched to extreme conditions.

No sea trip

They make the outward and homeward journey of over 14,000 miles by air and do not have the restful delights of a sea trip. Why within two days of arriving in Johannesburg they are due to play Southern Transvaal and from that moment the time table is recorded almost day by day in minutes.

Yes, this United tour of South Africa is an enormous undertaking and one that might well cause concern for the season that knocks on the door within a few weeks of their return to Tyneside.

21 months "season"

It means, in fact, taking the opening game of last season—August 18—a soccer spell with hardly a break of 21 months, until the end of season 1952-53.

And remember United do not receive any cash out of the tour.

A Wonder wandering for all who make the tour, but for the football of next season, a trip that might well have disastrous repercussions.

* * *

Even the national dailies knew that it was suicidal to embark on a tour.

United once more, the team presented Stan Seymour with a pen and pencil set to mark the occasion of the Boss' birthday on 16th May. On arrival in South Africa Jackie Milburn, still carrying an injury, was told he would be out for at least ten days.

Twenty-five thousand people turned up to watch our first game of the tour against Southern Transvaal. Unused to the strange atmospheric conditions and

United's full party pose in their snazzy 'water repellent Zenith jerkins' before jetting off. (See advertising poster in front.) In the next ten weeks the team were to sponsor many South African and international products.

lively ball, United were shocked into a 2-0 deficit very early in the game. Two goals from George Robledo and one from Hannah saved the blushes of the 500 Geordies who had come to acclaim 'their' team, and got us off to a good start. Next stop was to be Natal by train, and from there a quick flight to Cape Town for the third match in five days.

The tour was proving to be a tiring one for everybody. With only half of the games played, of the sixteen players in the party only Harvey had played in every game. There was great excitement when we went to play against Northern Rhodesia, with its large British community. A broadcast of the match went out in English and Afrikans. We won the game 6-1 with some unusual names on the score-sheet ... mine for instance! Plus a Bobby Cowell penalty and a rare goal from skipper Harvey.

We next played Eastern Transvaal whom Wolves had beaten 13-0 only the previous year. Playing Frank Brennan at centre-forward, we coasted to a 2-0 victory with the big-yin scoring one goal. It was while we were there that the FA back home announced that the Charity Shield match – Manchester United v Newcastle United – would take place on 24 September 1952. Another item of information that emerged from the FA meeting was that the following year's Cup Final was to be televised.

We suffered our only defeat of the tour against a selected South African squad at the Rand Stadium in what was described in the local papers as a 'Test Match'. It was here we were beaten 5-3, thanks to chasing a lively ball on a bone hard pitch.

We did have some humorous incidents in the land of Zulus and Safari Parks. On one day-trip we passed through Kruger National Park, the biggest game preserve in the world, and our cars pulled up at the first outpost. During

They were fun games, with United doing just sufficient to win as well as entertain.

At half-time at the Rand Stadium, big Frank thought he would level things out by plonking the ball in a pail of water which Milburn sat on during the interval. We played better in the second half, but ten weeks' hard slog in boiling temperatures had taken its toll, and we were looking forward to coming back home.

supper, one of the guards said that the wild animals often jumped over the stockade. As we were sleeping there, some of the lads looked uneasy.

I was sharing with Alf McMichael, and about midnight awoke to find Alf shaking me by the shoulder and saying: 'Come on, Charlie, there's a wild animal at the door'. Trembling, we tried to light the oil lamp. Outside we could hear grunting noises and scratching. The kraal we were sleeping in had no windows, so we could not look outside.

Alf said: 'I am gonna make a dash for help, Charlie.' But I blocked his escape, saying: 'There is no way you are going anywhere near that door and leaving me all alone with a lion scratching around outside.' Eventually, the noise ceased and we settled down to a fitful sleep. Next morning we were out and about telling of our great escape from a lion or

I was all right this time with Big Frank to protect me.

some other such wild beast. As we finished our story, there were tremendous gusts of laughter from Stan Seymour and trainer Norman Smith – *they* had been the lion scratching at the door.

We returned to the UK leg-weary, jet-lagged, and in need of a good rest. But we barely had a week before we had to report back to St James' Park to start all over again. From the opening day of the previous season until the end of the 1952/53 season, we would have had a soccer spell of twenty-one months with hardly a break. There was concern in the press that United would pay dearly for our strength-sapping trek in the next campaign. The cost of our tour, £16,000, had been paid by the South African FA. We had played sixteen games and lost only once.

For our first practice match we had to play with borrowed boots as ours were still 'deap-sea' somewhere near the Bay of Biscay. Ground prices went up for the new season from one shilling and sixpence to one shilling and ninepence. Season ticket holders had to pay £7 instead of the usual five.

We began the season badly, some might say predictably, by gaining only seven points from our first eight games. Milburn returned to play against West Brom on New Year's Day, after a long lay-off through injury. The only memorable thing about that game was that someone's chimney went on fire down Leazes Terrace, belching thick, black smoke across the pitch, making visibility virtually nil. Some wag in the crowd shouted: 'Set a'haad to another bugger,' as we coughed and spluttered to a 5-3 defeat. Milburn, Mitchell and Davies got our consolation goals.

After coming back from South Africa, I had been hailed in the press as an automatic choice for first team inclusion. Having been feted out there rather like heart-throbs and film stars, I do remember a rather eventful game for the Reserves against Blackpool's second team that brought me back to earth with a bump. The match at St James' was described in the *Football Chronicle* under a banner heading that screamed:

CROWE EMERGENCY 'KEEPER FOR UNITED

It then went on:

'Three changes in Newcastle United Reserves' team entertaining Blackpool this afternoon brought in Crowe for Stoddart at left-half and Alex Tait on the right-wing for Foulkes who moved to inside-right to the exclusion of Hadrick. Newcomer Keery had the spotlight all to himself, the ex-Shrewsbury Town player making his home debut in a Newcastle team that was as follows: R. Robinson, Sid Hutton, Cahill, Joe Harvey, Greener, Charlie Crowe, Alex Tait, Foulkes, Tulip, Keery and George Luke.

'Within five minutes United suffered their first misfortune when Blackpool's Drurie placed a long through ball which Hepton ran on to at the same time as goalie Robinson advanced. From the tussle, Robinson emerged with a bleeding right hand and had to leave the field. Crowe took over in goal.

'In the 12th minute, Crowe won his first round of applause by tipping Mudie's 25-yard drive out of harm's way. In between Newcastle attacks, Crowe was introducing some unorthodox antics into his goalkeeping. The main thing was he was succeeding … Crowe fell on a ball from Drurie 22 yards out. Later he dropped the ball and every spectator laughed. Crowe, taking it all in good fun, left Hutton to rescue him. "Best laugh I've had in years," was Stan Seymour's comment, as Crowe took to dribbling the ball outside the area and sometimes even heading clear. Score – Newcastle 1 Blackpool 2.'

I was a comic goalie for the day.

The Third Round of the FA Cup saw us at home to Swansea. A massive crowd of 63,499 turned out to cheer United on their way to what they hoped would be a hat-trick of Cup wins. Getting his first taste of Cup-tie soccer was a young Bob Stokoe, preferred to Harvey at right-half. Joe Harvey put on a brave face, saying: 'I was Bob's best man at his wedding and wished him luck then – the same goes now.' But in almost a repeat of the West Brom game, the referee brought the match to a halt after only eight minutes. There was no sooty smoke this time, only a grey blanket of fog that had been wrapped around Newcastle for days. The Swansea team booked into the Rex Hotel at Whitley Bay where they stayed until the Wednesday when another great crowd of 61,064 paid money for the second time – there was no refund after the first postponement.

We managed to beat Swansea 3-0 with a side that included Vic Keeble at centre-forward for an injured Milburn. Keeble scored twice with Reg Davies getting the other. Before the replayed game, the draw for the next round was made, fortune favouring us for a second time this time with a home draw against Second Division, Rotherham.

Our treatment room at St James' on the Monday prior to the Rotherham game resembled a casualty ward. Only *four* players reported fit enough to play, and of these, Keeble, still officially a soldier, was playing for the Army in a mid-week game. Jackie Milburn was definitely ruled out, but other regulars were expected to be able to play on the Saturday.

Rotherham, a side that included eight pitmen, brought fourteen players in their party for a three-day stay at the Park

Newcastle's Bob Stokoe never dreamed that he would one day manage a jubilant Sunderland team to win the 1973 FA Cup Final.

Hotel, Tynemouth. On the right-wing was a part-time miner called Len White who had recently played for a Football Association eleven.

We began the game hesitatingly, and at half-time there was no score. The awkward-looking Keeble (someone once joked that they couldn't even get shotwire to bend to that shape) managed to knock in a goal in the sixty-third minute, but in doing so he was injured and spent the rest of the game limping. Within five minutes Rotherham were level, a signal for the whole of our defence, apart from Cowell, to crumble, enabling the visitors to score two more. Our supporters were streaming out of the ground long before the final whistle, prompting Stan Seymour to say: 'That's that. Now we use the breathing space to build for fresh triumphs.'

Newcastle United continued their search for new talent, causing a national daily newspaper columnist to write a headline that proclaimed:

IS A GREAT TEAM CRACKING UP?
Their Honeymoon is Over!

It went on:

'Jackie Milburn is a nice fellow. Bobby Cowell is a nice fellow. George Robledo is a nice fellow. Joe Harvey, Charlie Crowe, Tommy Walker … all nice pleasant lads. They don't profess to be much more than professional players, but at that, they are very very good. They play for Newcastle United, and I think they are getting a rough deal.

'Fit or unfit, they never appear to be sure of a place in the side from one week to the next. Since the season started, this team of glorious Cup memory has been chopped around until it is almost mincemeat.

'Unbeaten in the Cup for two seasons, Newcastle United lost a Fourth Round Cup-tie to Rotherham, on their own near impregnable St James' Park. The call went out immediately that there would be some changes made, and the club is scouring two countries for players. As though a Cup-tie had never been lost before! Small wonder that two League games since have been lost.

'This at a time when United have such high-class players as Stokoe, Davies, Mulgrew, Casey, McMichael, Keeble and Foulkes, in addition to those already mentioned. Seven internationals on the books – a complete international forward line available.

'No club in the country has as many high-class experienced players. Now, any team in the country can lose a Cup-tie, even my 1953 sweethearts Manchester United. Of the hundreds of clubs entered for the Cup each year, only *one* stays undefeated.

'The long honeymoon for Newcastle is over. The individual brilliance of their players has carried them through two wonderful years. But this season there seems to have been too many changes merely for the sake of change. If you think we are kicking them when they are down, all right, but we are only trying to kick them up again. A successful Newcastle United is a shot in the arm for football.

'At the moment, Newcastle could, with luck, win the championship. They could, with the other kind of luck, find themselves back in the Second Division. Let the directors take a long look at Arsenal, for instance, understand that there is something known as patience in football, and give some of their players a longer chance to settle down to the football they CAN play, and bring us back some of those impassioned, flaming moments of football fury that have stunned us in the past. And let them start now.'

You must remember that by now we no longer had the services of the Robledo brothers who had departed to play for Coco Cola, a Chilean team.

Vic Keeble leads a party of Newcastle players and officials across the tarmac to board a plane for a close-season tour: From left: Keeble, Simpson, McMichael, Len White, Wilf Taylor a director, Lackenby, Crowe, Stokoe and Mitchell.

So when the crucial Easter programme arrived we were still not out of relegation trouble. Other clubs having a dog-fight at the bottom of the table were: Derby, Man City, Stoke, Sheffield Wed, Liverpool and Chelsea. One crucial game was at home to Manchester United at St James' when the following teams lined up. Newcastle: Simpson, Cowell, McMichael, Harvey, Brennan, Crowe, Walker, Mulgrew, Milburn, Hannah and Mitchell. Manchester United: Olive, McNulty, Byrne, Carey, Chilton, Whitefoot, Violett, Pearson, Aston, Taylor and Rowley.

This is how that match was described in the *Sunday Sun*:

'Newcastle United can still go down into the Second Division on the form shown in yesterday's home defeat by Manchester United, for despite having most of the ball, the forward play was once more not strong enough to burst the proverbial paper bag.

Billy Foulkes joined United from Chester and was awarded a Welsh cap within days of signing. Native of Merthyr Vale.

'Tommy Taylor, the young forward signed by Manchester from Barnsley after Newcastle had decided not to bid, got the two goals which sent Newcastle officials, players and 38,000 spectators scurrying for a *Football Chronicle* to scan the revised League relegation placings.

'It was a tantalising day for Newcastle director Stan Seymour. Having seen United reach virtual safety last Saturday, he stopped with the Reserves on Monday and saw them beat Liverpool 7-1 to end a long unsuccessful run.

'At thirty-six years of age, Manchester Utd skipper John Carey still looked the most complete footballer on the park. Strong enough in the tackle to keep a firm brake on Hannah, he virtually strolled though the game, always to sound and constructive purpose.

'Both Harvey and Crowe strove desperately and well to inspire some thrust from the three inside forwards. Brennan was another player with a heart-breaking view of Newcastle's impotent finish.

'The visitors virtually carried their 4th choice goalkeeper Olive who was very shaky most of the way. But another League debutante, Denis Viollet at outside right, gave a fine display. Goal scorers were Taylor (2) and Mitchell.'

Johnny Carey, on left, leads out a Manchester United team at Old Trafford in the 1950s. Carey went on to be a successful manager at Everton and Blackburn.

And so the 1952/53 season ended on a sour note, but highlights had been Scottish caps for Frank Brennan; and an Irish captaincy for Alf McMichael. Jackie Milburn had lost his place in the England team to Nat Lofthouse of Bolton Wanderers. We went on to play in a tournament especially arranged to celebrate Coronation year, featuring top English and Scottish clubs. Before these games got under way, Stan Seymour announced that Newcastle had signed teetotal, non-smoking Jimmy Scoular from Portsmouth for a club record fee of £25,000. It was also stated that Scoular was to take over the captaincy straight away, and that Joe Harvey's main role in the future was to be Reserve and Youth team coach.

This caused Jackie Milburn to say later:

'Seymour signed Scoular to take over as captain – I don't know why – things were never the same with Joe Harvey out of the team. His credentials in comparison to Scoular – phew! Jimmy was a nice fella, but he was the start of cliques, cos he was Scottish, and you got a few of them knocking around together.

'Scoular was a good player, but he wasn't what we were used to at Newcastle. Mainly we were all local lads who'd got together after the war.'

JACKIE'S GOAL —BEST I'VE EVER SEEN

"GOLDEN GOALS." THAT'S THE TITLE OF JACKIE MILBURN'S BOOK THAT IS TO MAKE HISTORY FOR THE "MAGPIES," FOR IT WILL BE THE FIRST-EVER SOCCER STORY TO BE WRITTEN AND PUBLISHED BY A GALLOWGATE PLAYER.

I look forward to reading his story.

I have played against the Tyneside favourite and, indeed, with him over the years and many are the golden goals I have seen him net.

My mind goes back to that season when United gave my old team, Portsmouth, the K.O. in the Cup. I recall the hat-trick Jackie scored against us. And in so doing I remember a wonder goal—he got two —for United at Wembley to beat Blackpool and bring the trophy to Tyneside.

Just timing

Little did I visualise in those days that I would be playing along with Milburn for United to see the most amazing goal I have ever witnessed to date. It was that near 40 yards winner in the first half against Preston at Gallowgate last Saturday.

How did it all happen? To me the answer is simple. It was perfection in timing. It was not the power behind the drive, but the manner in which the contact was accomplished.

After the match goalkeeper Else told me how he was deceived. "It just looked like a feeble lob to me. But before I knew anything about it the ball was resting in the back of the net."

It was normal in the 1950s for footballers to write for local newspapers. When Newcastle United tried to sign a 15-year-old Bobbie Charlton, one of the carrots they dangled in front of him was the promise of a weekly column in the Newcastle Journal.

Jackie autographs his book, Golden Goals, in 1957.

WHETHER JACKIE MILBURN SHOULD BE AT OUTSIDE-RIGHT OR CENTRE-FORWARD FOR NEWCASTLE UNITED WILL GO DOWN AS ONE OF THE GREATEST CONTROVERSIES IN TYNESIDE'S SOCCER HISTORY.

AS a winger, Milburn is not wasted. While playing centre-forward he has learned to be more quick thinking and more progressive in his play, something which he needed before, when he originally held the position.

Given more direct thrust from the inside men instead of the exasperating tip-tap crossfield play, he can be a most dangerous winger in the game. He has the talent to draw a defence and position himself to most types of ball. He is adaptable to the interchange of positions. His ability to keep a defence guessing is grand to watch, as he can move either way and use both feet, an asset to any man on the wing. —T. Alderson, St. Anthonys.

UNDOUBTEDLY Milburn's place is on the wing. He is a maker of goals as well as a scorer; remember the goals he made for Robledo. The natural place for a maker of goals is on the wing and he can still score the odd one.

Think of the hard knocks he received as leader, and the games he missed through injuries. United can't afford to have such a valuable player on the injured list and this risk is not nearly so great if he is played on the wing. —M. METCALF, Morpeth.

"Hard knocks he received."

MILBURN is one of the speediest and most useful wingers in the business, but he should now be played at centre-forward, as goals are vital, and Jackie is the man for that job. — A. E. MARSHALL, Lowes Barnes.

JACKIE MILBURN

IT is true Milburn has played international football on the wing, but unfortunately Newcastle have not the inside forwards who can take advantage of his immaculate service and precision centres. So until these positions are adequately filled, I say play Jackie in the middle.—L. ARROWSMITH, Gateshead.

THERE is definitely only one answer to this question— Milburn must be put back in the centre. It was a mistake in the first place to move him, shown clearly by the fact that the forward line has not come up to the standard of last season.

We know he has done well on the wing this season but the fact is Newcastle need him as centre-forward.
J. A. TOMLINSON, Browney Colliery

JACKIE MILBURN is a great centre-forward but an even greater winger. His direct methods and cutting in for goal, coupled with dynamite shots with both feet from any angle, plus perfect centres and corners make him one of the greatest wingers of today.—W. WALLS, Low Fell.

"Shots in both feet."

I, a Scotsman, having watched football for years both in England and Scotland, vote for Milburn at centre forward, he being the sort of leader we spectators love to watch, able to make and take chances. —William McDOWALL, Throckley.

"Spectators love to watch."

He knows his best position

I THINK that Jackie should be given the opportunity of choosing his position. In the Press recently he stated that he had a preference for outside-right. He is playing such wonderful football just now, so why return him to the middle and cramp his style.

On the wing he has been playing with renewed confidence, moving about with the greatest of ease instead of being shackled by three half-backs.

Finally the club should get someone to convert his wonderful centres and those accurate corner kicks, which should have given United a bundle of goals, but instead they have been wasted.—E. HALL, South Bank.

There was always talk of from which position did Jackie Milburn perform better: centre-forward or outside-right? An Evening Chronicle poll brought in the these letters.

That year saw us football players get a great pay rise – from fourteen pounds a week to fifteen pounds a week! But this was only a maximum, and many clubs paid far less. At Newcastle, twenty-two players were on the £15 maximum when the 1953/54 season got under way.

The first game of the new season was a real appetiser, a local derby against Sunderland. The Wearsiders, living up to their reputation as the 'Bank of England' team, fielded three costly close-season signings: Ray Daniel, Jimmy Cowan and Billy Elliott. The gates were opened earlier than usual, 12.30 pm, to allow the crowds plenty of time to take their place. Pre-match entertainment was provided by the band of the 4th and 5th Royal Northumberland Fusiliers.

Milburn was selected at outside-right for the first time in two seasons. Two minutes into the game, Shackleton put Sunderland ahead. Scoular was injured soon afterwards and was in pain for the rest of the game. Milburn constantly left the opposition standing with solo thrusts on goal. Although Jackie didn't score, he had an excellent game and made goals for Keeble and Mitchell to win the match 2-1.

With no Scoular and with Joe Harvey also missing, there was a dressing room meeting ending in a ballot, and I was told by Milburn and Mitchell that I had been voted club captain. By then I was re-established in the first team as regular left-half. And I have never felt more proud than on the first Saturday that I led the lads out on to St James' Park.

As a team we were beginning to look good again, showing a consistency that left us afraid of no-one. For a match against Liverpool fielding Bob Paisley at left-half, we were again unchanged, and showed a bit of class by taming Liverpool 4-0. This was our third consecutive home win, and it sent the statisticians scurrying to their books as far back as 1929 to recall such a feat. But a home game with Bolton even without their international centre-forward Nat Lofthouse was the game we chose to slip back into slipshod ways and we were beaten 3-2.

On a week's special training at Blackpool, Bob Stokoe missed his footing on the stairway of a big department store, fell down half a dozen steps, and wrenched his knee. The injury signalled the recall of Scoular into the side against West Brom at home. The Throstles, playing by far the best football in Division One, trounced us 7-3.

At an annual general meeting, United announced a loss of £38,619. Transfer fees together with players' wages amounted to £85,970. Stan Seymour, voted chairman of the board for the first time,

I was never more proud than when leading the black and whites on to St James' Park.

assured supporters that they 'would get the class of football they rightly deserved.'

Back to their inconsistent ways, United broke a thirty-two-year-old record, this time for *losing* three consecutive home games, when they lost 3-1 to Spurs.

This defeat panicked Seymour into making seven changes including moving Jackie Milburn to lead the attack. But shuffling the pack did not produce the required magic to beat Sheffield Wednesday, and after a 3-0 drubbing we found ourselves sixth to bottom of a League table that we had looked like heading at the outset.

Again players were unhappy at being left out, and Hannah and McMichael asked for transfers. The Irish captain's left-back position was now being filled by hard-tackling Ron

Ron Batty was two-footed with a preference for the left flank. West Stanley born, he joined United in 1944. Height 5ft 8ins; weight 11st 10lbs.

Batty, who had played the role of understudy for so long. McMichael commented: 'It is not in my best interests as an international to be out of League football.'

Following our *sixth* consecutive home defeat – 2-0 by Huddersfield – Stan Seymour left the ground after only twenty minutes play, saying to a *Newcastle Journal* reporter:

'I hope it will be understood that I shall act in the firm opinion, with the interests of Newcastle always put first, that the club is greater than the individual … any individual.'

The following week, in a seven-hour spell, Seymour bought two new forwards: local lad Alan Monkhouse and Ivor Broadis, much travelled English international who landed at Newcastle via Carlisle, Sunderland and Manchester City. The twenty-nine-year-old Broadis cost Seymour £20,000. When asked if that was the end of his recruiting drive, Seymour commented evasively: 'Who knows? It depends on the players.' Ivor Broadis scored two goals on his home

Ivor Broadis was a skilful inside forward with a powerful shot. He won 14 caps for England but could never seem to fit into a United team, making 51 appearances and scoring 20 goals. Wrote for a local newspaper.

debut against Cardiff whom we beat 3-0.

Alan Monkhouse had been signed from Millwall for £11,500 as a left-winger. After Norman Smith had brought him into the dressing room and introduced Alan to us, he mentioned to me that George Stobbart, who was now at Millwall, had suggested that he ask me to show him around.

Monkhouse and I trained together and when doing some laps around St James' he turned and said: 'You know, Charlie, I can't really understand why Newcastle bought me – I'm not a very good player.' I thought at first that he was joking, but I could see he was deadly serious. He made his debut against Cardiff at the same time as Ivor Broadis. When the game started I found Alan with a pass which he collected, only to run straight through the Cardiff right-back, Stitfall, knocking him to the ground. Stitfall looked up and said to me: 'Who the hell is he?' Alan never made the grade as a winger but he later developed into a strong bustling old-fashioned centre-forward, scoring 11 goals in 23 games for us. Years later when talking to George Stobbart about Monkhouse, he said that the Newcastle scout had made a mistake and that the wrong player had been signed.

George Stobbart was a Pegswood lad. Seen in centre here in 1948 flanked by Andy Donaldson and myself.

England took on Hungary at Wembley on 25th November 1953 fielding Newcastle cast-off Ernie Taylor getting a belated first cap for his country. But even Ernie's wiles could not rescue England from a Hungarian side that gave the Englishmen a lesson in the way football should now be played.

Stan Seymour must have been impressed with the Magyar style of playing a centre-forward 'deep' behind the rest of the attack, because that was the way he and new coach Joe Harvey asked Milburn to play in our next game against Arsenal. Said one of the Gunner's defenders: 'Newcastle tried to play a Hungarian rhapsody.'

Newcastle, after being drawn against Lancashire Combination League team Wigan in the Third Round of the FA Cup, were laid at 12-1, with Wolves the 9-1 favourites. Wigan's manager said: 'Wigan has gone crazy over the cup-tie against the famous Newcastle United. The boys are eager to intensify training.'

Thanks to our abysmal League form, we went into the Christmas games only five places above bottom team, Liverpool, who already looked doomed.

Ernie Taylor (bottom row 2nd right) and Jackie Milburn appeared together in an England shirt in a Festival of Britain game against Portugal in 1951. Milburn is standing next to Alf Ramsey from whom he took over as manager of Ipswich in 1963

when Ramsey went on to be England's manager in the run-up to the 1966 World Cup which would feature two of Jackie's relatives: Bob and Jack Charlton.

Milburn was dropped from the team to play fellow strugglers Middlesbrough, and thanked Seymour for it. It was Jackie's first break in an ever-present run during that season. Milburn announced to the sporting press:

'I am glad I was dropped. It was a refresher to sit in the stand. I felt I could see how I may be able to alter my game to recover the form I found on the wing in the opening games of the season. There is no danger of me being unsettled at being left out. I expect I'll be in the Central League side against Manchester United next week. But, at twenty-nine, I don't mean to be dropped by United again for a long time once I'm in again.'

Sunderland were also in the relegation zone, and when Jackie was dropped into the Reserves they made discreet enquiries about his availability. They had a crisis at centre-forwards themselves: Trevor Ford had gone to Cardiff, and the Wearsiders resorted to fielding Welsh international centre-half Ray Daniel as a leader of the attack. Although Milburn might have welcomed the short trip from Tyne to Wear,

It was often said that it would take a tank to stop JET Milburn when in full flight. Here he christens a tank 'Wor Jackie' for the Army at Fenham Barracks.

Seymour made it clear that a move was out of the question.

Back in the first team on New Year's Day, Jackie did his first-footing at the expense of Blackpool, scoring both goals in a 2-0 win. Ted Goodier, Wigan's manager, was at that match and afterwards told a *Newcastle Journal* reporter:

'I know my team will be beaten 11-0 next Saturday, and I changed my mind about bringing the rest of the team today in case it frightened them. The Wigan station-master says he will have a red carpet ready if we draw.'

No-one was fooled by this piece of pre-match kidology. Wigan were Combination leaders and had already beaten Hereford and Scarborough in earlier rounds, and with our present in-and-out form, we could never feel confident whatever the opposition.

As in previous years, Buxton was chosen for a week's special training before the Cup game. Seymour picked this game to experiment with the team, and dropped Bobby Cowell, with Ron Batty switching from left to right full-back. But it was the forward-line formation which was the most astonishing. Milburn, a makeshift centre-forward, but obviously more at ease on the right wing, was picked to play inside-left, with Alan Monkhouse brought in to lead the attack.

Wigan gave us an almighty fright at St James' Park where Broadis scored early in the game. But the Lancashire side came back to lead 2-1. It needed a ferocious Milburn drive to level the game, draw the match, and set everyone wondering where the replay would be held. Wigan's dressing rooms had been

Still the pin-ups of the football world, Newcastle United players were sought the world over for their photos – even followed into the showers. Brennan, Milburn, Cowell and me in the buff at Bloomfield Road, Blackpool in 1953.

burned down the previous April. The Wigan Rugby club offered their ground, but Wigan FC were adamant that that their own Springfield Park, holding 31,000, was to be the venue for the replay the following Wednesday.

For this game, Newcastle relied on a side that looked a little more reliable. Cowell came back and Keeble replaced Monkhouse at centre-forward. An anonymous phone call sent Seymour scurrying over to Wigan. What he saw horrified him. He told the national press: 'It is terrible. The pitch is bad enough, but the facilities are dreadful. The game should have gone to the Rugby ground. It is like a wreck at the back of the pier! I have phoned several directors to ask them to stay at home rather than tackle this shambles.' The Wigan manager exploded: 'What do they expect? We lost all our accommodation in a fire. Newcastle are getting spoilt – nobody else has complained.'

Very few of the 6,000 tickets for the replay were taken up by United supporters, and only 300 fans booked for the special train that left Newbiggin by the Sea at 6.50 am on the morning of the match. Ticket touts were seen boarding the train at Newcastle Central with boxes full of half-crown tickets which they had hoped to sell for inflated prices. In the programme that day was an appeal for Wigan supporters not to barrack Newcastle United on account of 'eve-of-the-match ground controversy.' The 27,000 crowd did their best to lift the local team after we had gone into a commanding 2-0 lead, but we were relieved to hang on for a 3-2 victory which put us through to play an away tie against Burnley, a match that ended up as a 1-1 draw. In the replay at St James' it was level pegging right until the last ten minutes. The two Ashington men in opposition – Newcastle's Milburn and Burnley's Jimmy Adamson – collided going for a fifty-fifty ball near the Burnley goal.

THE Jackie MILBURN
ANGLE ON SOCCER

Mitchell in the star 'mould'

TODAY, in my focus on team positions, I arrive at the outside-left berth.

Tynesiders are fortunate in much more than other that they have seen Bobby Mitchell in action Soccer followers.

For, in my opinion, Bob is the best outside-left there has been since the end of the war.

According to managers, outside-left is the most difficult spot to fill, and the reason for this is the shortage of natural left-footers.

Indeed, the majority of British clubs have had to convert right-footed players into outside-lefts.

Craze for speed

These conversions have met with a certain amount of success, but unless a player has exceptional ability with two feet, or is a "great," it is the "natural" who invariably achieves the greatest success.

For control and accuracy in using the ball, "Mitch" is in the Matthews-Finney mould, and though players of this calibre are often criticised for holding the ball too long—and holding up team play—their records speak for themselves.

It is unfortunate that modern coaching methods seem to be ousting the ball players—because of the present craze for speed.

Bobby Mitchell is a "thinker" and studies the game very

during the 90 minutes lost the ball on only one occasion. This was certainly some feat!

Ve won 2—0. Walking off the field with Staniforth, whose tongue was hanging on the ground, he told me: "I've had some tough games—but never one like that."

'Mitch" and I were rather lazy trainers, and about the only time we put ourselves out in training sessions was when the ball was "on the go."

Bob's best friend was the ball, and for many an hour he practised ball control. This has certainly paid handsome dividends.

Another great left-winger, though with an opposite style to Mitchell, is New-castle-born Jimmy Mullen who has been with Wolver-hampton all his career.

Jimmy is not a great believer in the fancy stuff, but is fast and direct.

Milburn wrote a column for various papers – he said that was his 'pocket money'. Here he gives his verdict on an old pal, Bob Mitchell.

Jackie went down, Jimmy pleaded an accident, but the referee gave a penalty. Mitchell made no mistake and we marched on into Round Five.

The Round Five game was to be against First Division leaders, West Brom. Vic Buckingham, their manager, commented in the *News of the World*:

'We realise that our Cup opponents are capable of very good displays, but we shall not be worrying about what they can do. We think this is to be *our* year in the League and Cup.'

Buckingham's optimism proved to be well founded as his team went into a 2-0 lead. United fought back and were dominating the game when the final whistle blew with the score at 3-2 in West Brom's favour, ending our 1954 hopes of a return to Wembley. Said Seymour, apparently undismayed by the display: 'We are proud of the fight the boys made and the shock they gave a very good opposition. We shall field the same side against Charlton on Thursday.'

And that was the end of us and the FA Cup for that season. But we were still locked in a relegation struggle that featured all the North East's big guns: Newcastle, Sunderland and Middlesbrough in the bottom five of the League. Liverpool were five points adrift and virtually sure to go down, it was simply a case of who went with them. (Only two clubs were relegated in those days.)

For the home game against Sheffield United, Alan Monkhouse was brought back and scored a hat-trick. Milburn got a goal, and we were practically safe after a 4-1 win.

Bob Stokoe was the next player to ask for a transfer. He had already tried to

Ronnie Simpson was a reflex goalie. Here I shepherd the ball to him in a game at St James' Park. Just see Bob Stokoe in rear.

get away in 1953. This time he was unhappy about being played as Brennan's deputy when the big Scot had been injured. He told any sporting reporter who would listen: 'I am prepared to sign for about any First or Second Division side, as long as it is understood that I move to right-half, the position for which I was trained. On general grounds, too, I should like to try my luck elsewhere.'

Seymour replied: 'Stokoe has forced our hands by his agitation for a move, and he is on the list.' It was thought that a price of around £10,000 was asked for Stokoe. The next week against Derby County Reserves, United fielded five unhappy players who had asked for transfers: Bob Stokoe, George Hannah, Billy Foulkes, Ron Batty and Reg Davies. Vic Keeble got a hat-trick that day as the 'stiffs' won 3-1.

Mathematically, we could still be relegated, but in a game played over the Easter period we beat Sheffield Wednesday 3-1 to assure our status for another year. Ivor Broadis, the only Newcastle player chosen for the 1954 English World Cup squad, was unable to get into the Newcastle side that day.

As a very disappointing season for us came to a close, West Brom who had knocked us out of the Cup, went on to beat Preston 3-2 in the Final, but failed to do the Double as Wolves took the Championship. Middlesbrough was the unlucky North East side to slip into the Second Division, together with Liverpool.

Having shown a massive loss on the season, the Newcastle board adopted a penny-pinching attitude and dropped Ronnie Simpson's wage to £13. This so antagonised the Scottish goalkeeper, who had missed only three games in two seasons, that he made the following statement in the *Newcastle Journal*:

'It would appear that I am singled out of all the regular League team players for this wage cut. If I do re-sign for next season I will ask for a transfer.'

Two other players, Foulkes and White (the latter now working part-time in a Tyneside pit), also took pay cuts. As usual, Seymour was able to justify the board's action: 'We are adopting an incentive scheme whereby players whose play warrants top money will get it, whether in the first or second team.'

After Jackie Milburn left it was Len White who proved the scourge of opposition goalkeepers.

If Ronnie Simpson failed to negotiate the ball then bet your boots that Bobby Cowell would pop up on the line to clear the danger. Seen here playing against Arsenal.

HOWAY THE LADS IT'S WORS AGAIN, 1954/55

Newcastle players right up until Cup Final day in 1955 did not know who would make it on to the Wembley pitch to play Man City. For a long time this United eleven, seen at the Hawthorns against West Brom, looked as though they could be in with a shout of being picked. One player was sure he wouldn't play at Wembley. That was Ivor Broadis, seated 2nd left, who had seen his name on the top of a list marked 'Open to transfer'. Back left: Jimmy Scoular, Bobby Cowell, Ronnie Simpson, Bob Stokoe, Bob Mitchell. Front: Jackie Milburn, Ivor Broadis, Alf McMichael (captain for the day), Len White, Charlie Crowe and George Hannah. Note the old-fashioned boots and 'caser' football.

Before the new 1954/55 season got under way, Derby County stepped in with an offer for unsettled Bob Stokoe. Events were to dictate that a Stokoe move was out of the question. Frank Brennan was *not* included in the Probable side against the Possibles in a trial match. The black and white side that day was: Simpson, Cowell, McMichael, Scoular, Lackenby, Crowe, Milburn, Broadis, Keeble, Hannah and Mitchell.

Seymour rushed up to Scotland in an attempt to sign Partick Thistle's centre-half Jim Davidson, but when a figure of £20,000 was mentioned, Seymour backed out of the bidding. Back on Tyneside, Frank Brennan was mystified at this undignified scramble to sign a centre-half. At over 300 games, the amiable Scot had played far more matches for United than any of his contemporaries. 'I am quite fit and hoping for another five years in first-class football,' said Frank. 'I am signed up for the coming season and have made no move towards leaving Newcastle United.'

Frank Brennan was one of United's most consistent players. He made the mistake of opening up a couple of Sportswear shops that might have been seen as a threat to the ones owned by Stan Seymour.

Two of United's best-loved players, Jackie Milburn and Bobby Cowell, celebrated their 250th appearance for the club in a game against West Brom. Then Frank Brennan came back into the team as we completed an early double over Aston Villa, winning 2-0 with goals from Milburn and Mitchell.

After seven games had been played we shared first place in the League with Wolves and Manchester United. There was a growing feeling in the North East that this Newcastle squad, playing attractive and efficient football, could be in line for further honours. This proved wishful thinking as we threw away a 2-0 lead over Leicester to lose the match 3-2. Frank Brennan, obviously upset over all the speculation over his future, chose this day to play one of his most untidy games for Newcastle, sending Seymour hurrying off on another talent-spotting exercise.

The 'Boro signed a former Geordie lad, Charlie Wayman, from Southampton in an attempt to lift themselves from the bottom of the Second Division. They also came across to Tyneside with an open cheque book in an attempt to lure Frank Brennan to bolster a woefully weak defence. Big Frank refused to go. With Milburn tried again at centre-forward, and without Brennan, we lost a derby match at Roker Park by 4-2, sending the Wearside team clear at the top of the First Division. That game was described by sports writer Neville Holtham, under the heading:

UNITED MADE A SAD PICTURE

'Gleeful Sunderland partisans had all the laughs in a swaying, sweltering 66,654 crowd at Roker Park on Saturday. Newcastle beaten 4-2 and Sunderland going top of the First Division in the process – what could be better?

'To make the day complete, thrill-a-second Soccer had been controlled masterfully by Mr Arthur Ellis. Oh, yes, there was needle. That it never reached any dangerous stage could be laid simply to the referee's firmness.

'Sunderland's full strength side was speedy, thrustful and full of pep. Nothing classic, yet they had a solid look of competence. Maybe it is too early yet to talk of honours, but if this eleven can be kept together as often as possible, Sunderland should be knocking hard when April 1955 comes around.

'To a Tynesider like myself, this first view of Newcastle was a little saddening. Their backs were constantly harried by match-winning wingers. They were weak down the centre, and challenge at inside forward never came. Nevertheless, United had two of the game's best players in Bobby Mitchell and Charlie Crowe. Had Milburn been able to head in Mitchell's centre in the first quarter of an hour, matters might have been different.'

Seymour lost no time in enlisting a centre-half, and paid £22,000 for twenty-two-year-old Scot Bill Paterson who had been playing for Doncaster Rovers. Said Rovers' manager, Peter Doherty, with typical Irish blarney: 'Bill Paterson will gain Scotland caps with Newcastle United.'

On Paterson's signing, Seymour said: 'Stokoe now has the chance to fight for the wing-half place he desires.'

In an eventful match at home to Spurs, our defence, with Paterson making his debut, was all over the place, and the game ended in a high-scoring 4-4 draw. Our goalie was hurt and Jimmy Scoular took over in nets. This was the

Arthur Ellis was one of England's best and most respected referees. He later appeared on TV's It's a Knockout with Eddie Waring.

game I chose to score only my *second* goal for United in 132 appearances. And Spurs right-back Alf Ramsey after the game said: 'This is the worst playing surface in the First Division!'

A Newcastle United Shareholders' Association meeting, chaired by Mr E.C. Pringle, said that a letter should be sent to club directors requesting the appointment of a full-time manager. It was also felt that it should not be the duty of a club chairman (Stan Seymour) to act as manager as well. A query also arose regarding Middlesbrough coming to ask for Frank Brennan's signature when the player knew nothing about it. It seemed that both clubs had agreed on a figure of £12,000.

I didn't score all that many goals for Newcastle United so here is the one against Spurs when we won 7-0. Alf Ramsey stands helpless.

On 26th January 1955, the Newcastle board issued a statement to the effect that Brennan had *never* been for transfer, and that he would be retained by Newcastle and given the match practice needed for him to continue with his valuable service to the club.

The whole Brennan episode had cast a huge shadow over the Gallowgate ground. But there was never a doubt that the Geordie team had the character to forget the in-fighting and concentrate on the imminent Cup-tie against Brentford. The London team's manager, Bill Dodgin, was a much-travelled Gateshead man whose brother Norman had figured in a fine Newcastle team during the war. Another local connection from the same era was Pegswood-born centre forward George Stobbart. 'Stobbs', who had knocked in fifteen goals already that season for Brentford, joked: 'I'm hoping that I've got a trick or two up my sleeve which may put Bob Stokoe off once or twice.'

Dodgin said: 'I am bringing my lads up to Whitley Bay for a few days. Brentford people are thrilled by the prospect of meeting the Magpies in

Frank Brennan always tried to shrug off that 'stopper' centre-half tag. The craggy Scot liked nothing better than surging upfield.

the Cup – it has whetted their appetite for a sight of top-quality play.'

The Manchester referee was put on the spot even before the game began. He had to spin a coin to see which side changed from their traditional black shorts into white.

Having seemingly backed down over the Brennan issue, Seymour gave further ground by appointing a new manager, Dougald Livingstone, still coaching in Belgium with one year of a five-year contract to run.

Milburn had this to say of the new man:

'I only played under two managers: George Martin and a fella called Dougald Livingstone. You know what Livingstone did one day ... It sickened me. The most educated left foot I saw in my life was Bobby Mitchell's. The manager had us coaching at Fenham, and he drew a chalk mark on Bobby Mitchell's left boot, demonstrating how to side-foot a ball to the rest of us.

Training in the old days meant a leisurely jog around the perimeter of St James' Park. On a hard day we had to run around Newcastle's Town Moor.

Bobby Mitchell was known as 'Mitch the Magician' and was the idol of all the fans ... especially the ladies. He went on to score 113 goals in 408 games for United as well as winning three FA Cup medals. An honour he shared with Jackie Milburn and Bob Cowell.

"That's exactly the point where you catch it," he says.

'Whey the lads, like Frank Brennan and them, were looking at me, and we couldn't believe it! I mean … that's kids stuff. I says, "Hey, that's me finished with him. That's the end as far as I'm concerned." Everybody started to laugh about it, because they said Mitch's left foot was bloody dynamite! He could do anything with it … he could open a can of beans with his left foot, and … this chalk mark.

'Livingstone came from Sheffield Wednesday; he was the coach, and he'd been in Belgium. He was a nice fella, but a school teacher type. We were hard-bitten pros by the time he got there, and you expect somebody to be, not entirely ruthless, but the boss. You couldn't look up to fellas like this, and it caused cliques in the camp which we had never known. Up to then we had never known any cliques – gangs of three or four knocking about together, and this lot ignoring that lot. All this sort of thing seeped in then, and it was never the same when Joe Harvey left.

'Martin and Livingstone were the only two managers we had, because Seymour more or less ran things. It was run on promises. The club was run on promises. "Come on, lads, you win this one and I'll get the groceries in for you." Promises – just promises. The managers picked the team, but if the directors thought it wasn't right, they changed it straight away.'

I can vouch for the fact that Livingstone's coaching techniques bordered between the ludicrous and the dangerous. One visit to a gymnasium ended up with half the team being injured after jumping over hurdles and clambering up ropes suspended from the ceiling.

Doug Livingstone on right shuffled the United team as much as he did with Bob Mitchell, me, Bob Cowell and Ron Simpson.

Local bandleader George Evans, resident at the Oxford Galleries, composed a new waltz for his Geordie dancers. Entitled the 'Wembley Waltz', the lyrics of the song described the progress of Newcastle United in winning their two previous FA Cup Finals. George himself sang the song when the band were featured on the BBC North of England Home Service. The last two lines of the song went:

> 'We waltz to Wembley to see a bit of football,
> and watch Newcastle waltz off with the Cup.'

In the Cup-tie against Brentford, goals, which had looked an impossibility before half time, flew in after the interval as we scored three in a five-minute burst, including a rare goal from Bobby Mitchell's right foot.

Mitchell, 2nd left, swivels as he bangs in a right-foot shot that beats the Brentford 'keeper all ends up.

Eventually, we won 3-2 in a scrappy match. While we were involved in the glamour of the FA Cup, poor Frank Brennan was plodding his size elevens on the turf at Wallsend in a run-out for the Thirds against Heaton Stannington. After the game he said: 'So far as I am concerned, the whole thing is ended.'

We were drawn away to Nottingham Forest in the Fifth Round and were immediately made third favourites at 9-1 to win the Cup. Forest were in seventeenth position in the Second Division, but their manager Billy Walker was not dismayed by the draw, saying: 'On what I've seen of Newcastle they are nothing out of the ordinary, and I think we can beat them on our own pitch.' That pitch was only 400 yards away from the Notts County ground who were also due to play in the Fifth Round on the same day. With County's record gate standing at 49,000, and Forest's at 44,116, the streets of Nottingham, come kick-off time, were destined to be deserted.

Before then, United's board had a vote of No Confidence passed against them by the Shareholders. Estimated voting was 2,000 for and only three against. The board were also faced with team problems. English international Broadis was fit again but unable to command a place because of the good form of Reg Davies and George Hannah. Proving a good buy, Len White had played at centre-forward twelve times already that season, scoring eight goals from that position. Jackie Milburn roamed across the forward line playing in every position except outside-left.

Prior to the Cup game we all went to the Norbreck Hotel at Blackpool. Manager Livingstone told the *Daily Mail*:

'We had to get away from Newcastle, there is a foot of snow on the St James' pitch and the Fenham training ground. Conditions are more favourable at Blackpool. The team will not be decided till later.'

The Friday night before the game we trooped off to see the pantomime 'Jack and the Beanstalk ... on Ice'.

Livingstone brought back Bobby Cowell, who had been dropped in the previous game; Len White was included at centre-forward; and Vic Keeble got into the team at inside-left, to the exclusion of George Hannah who immediately asked for a transfer, saying: 'I don't think that it is fair that I should be dropped after playing in four games of which three were won. Plus I scored winning goals in two of these games, including a Cup-tie.'

As to the game itself, we had Milburn to thank for scoring an

A Newcastle United programme versus Leicester City in 1955.

equaliser four minutes from time in a game that we had looked like losing only a minute before. Livingstone blamed the ground for our lukewarm performance: 'Some of our boys were not too well suited by the conditions at Nottingham. Our replay team will not be named till I've seen the pitch.'

Stan Seymour seemed quite happy as he gave this statement to the *Newcastle Journal*:

'I am satisfied we can be in good form for Wednesday's replay. We did not play well, but we are still in the Cup, whereas Chelsea and Spurs went out to lower-class clubs.'

Thirty men were employed at St James' Park in an effort to get the pitch fit for the Wednesday, but the sudden fall of an extra six inches of snow set the game back till the following Monday.

For the 78th derby game against Sunderland, we had Broadis and Hannah returning to the side, while I was replaced by Tom Casey at left-half. I was suffering from an injury at the time. Keeble was played at centre-forward, with Milburn moving back to the right wing. Sunderland were without two of their stars: Len Shackleton was dropped into the Reserve team to play Blackhall Colliery, and Billy Bingham, their Irish international, was injured.

Sunderland's line-up was Fraser, Hedley, McDonald, Anderson, Daniel, Aitken, Kemp, Fleming, Purdon, Chisholm and Elliot.

Sunderland were also going well in the FA Cup. Here is Charlie Fleming leaping higher than Swansea's 'keeper to give the Wearside team a 1-0 victory in the Fifth Round replay.

Newcastle fielded Simpson, Cowell, Batty, Scoular, Stokoe, Casey, Milburn, Broadis, Keeble, Hannah and Mitchell.

A massive 61,550 crowd watched Sunderland beat us 2-1, with Milburn getting United's goal after moving back into the middle. It was a dismal show and the team had to lift itself or face a quick Cup exit. In the replayed Cup-tie with Forest, we scored two early goals through Mitchell and Keeble, but squandered the lead to end up 2-2 a score that was not improved on, even after extra time. It had already been agreed that, in the event of a draw, the next venue would be decided by the spin of a coin. Stan Seymour shouted 'Heads' and kept the tie at Newcastle.

Livingstone shuffled the forward line around yet again for the second replay, bringing in Alan Monkhouse at centre-forward, switching Milburn to inside-left, and bringing in Casey and Hannah to replace Broadis and Keeble. This time Monkhouse more than paid his way by scoring the two goals that helped us beat Forest 2-1. But it was Milburn's match as he wandered across the park, the complete footballer, emerging to torment defenders with devastating bursts of spccd as hc laid on both goals. A heading in the following day's *Newcastle Journal* confirmed: 'MILBURN UNITED SCRAPE THROUGH.'

To me, one of the finest sights in football was Jackie Milburn in full flight, chasing a through ball, his shirt billowing out behind him. He was a matchwinner – we knew it, but more than that, the opposition knew it. After that game, a shattered Forest centre-half, McKinley, said to a listening reporter: 'My only worry about these cup-ties was that Newcastle would play Milburn at centre-forward.' The Forest captain, Tom Wilson, agreed: 'Only one man beat us, and he is Milburn.'

Above: Milburn wheels away as he watches the ball cross the Forest goal-line on a snow-covered pitch at Nottingham.

Left: Bobby Mitchell again gets on the goalscoring sheet, this time against Notts Forest in the FA Cup Fifth Round at St James'.

With the Sixth Round tie at Huddersfield only days away, Livingstone was still undecided about the team's format. 'I prefer to watch the men in training another day or two before choosing the Cup men,' he told a journalist.

Returning from a spying mission on which he had seen Huddersfield lose 4-0 at Preston, Joe Harvey said: 'If that Huddersfield form is true, Newcastle should win well ... but I have my doubts.'

Huddersfield who had lost their last five League matches had Newcastle on the wrack and looking totally beaten and trailing 1-0. It was Milburn who teed one up for Len White to drive home and book Newcastle's ticket for yet another replay.

Two North East teams had already booked their place in the semi-finals: Sunderland beating Wolves 2-0, and Third Division York winning with the only goal of the match against Notts County. Manchester City made up the trio waiting to see who would complete the semi-final quartette.

Hours before the tickets went on sale for the Huddersfield game, there was a queue of expectant fans snaking over one hundred yards out of the ground.

Wearing the number ten shirt, Milburn is thwarted here by Huddersfield goalie, Wheeler.

Although still dangerously close to the bottom of the League, we still attracted 52,380 supporters to see us get the better of Huddersfield at the second attempt. Two goals came in extra time, Mitchell scoring first before Keeble made sure of that vacant semi-final place.

The semi-final draw kept the two big North East clubs apart, kindling hopes of a Newcastle v Sunderland final. Our game against York, at Hillsborough, looked the easier one to forecast, but Sunderland, near the top of the table, were made joint favourites in the betting: 2-1 Sunderland; 2-1 Newcastle; 9-4 Manchester City; and 14-1 York.

Tickets for the semi against York went on sale at 5 pm on Tuesday 22nd March, and touts were soon selling half-crown tickets for £1. Mrs Nellie Storer was the first to arrive at 7.30 am. She was met by a snowstorm and a fleet of hot-dog sellers who did brisk business throughout the day. As the time drew near to open the turnstiles, men arriving from work took over from their wives, many of whom had endured a four-hour blizzard.

The Newcastle board took us back to the Golden Mile at Blackpool prior to the semi-final, combining training with pleasure. After we had come out at the end of a variety show, who should have joined our party but Jimmy James, the comedian, who had been appearing in the show. The telephone rang in the next room and Alec Mutch our physio went to answer it. When he came back his face was wreathed in smiles. 'You've got twin boys, Charlie.'

Jimmy James quipped: 'Well, then, Charlie, how many children had you when you left Newcastle?'

Still expecting a joke, I told him that I had two. 'Ah, then you are the only man I know who has come to Blackpool with two children and gone home with four.' I thought it was all a hoax 'cos in the nine-month run up with my wife Ruth's pregnancy there had never been any mention of twins. But sure enough there were twin boys Charles and Simon when I got back home on the Monday.

Ruth said that her original doctor had been present at the birth, and when the first baby arrived he said: 'Very good, Mrs Crowe, you have a little Charlie.' But then this other doctor who was tidying me up noticed that another baby was on the way. 'Oh, one more, Mrs Crowe,' he said, but I was so weary I just muttered, 'Go to Hell!' And that was Simon. It was Alec Mutch's wife who rang the team at Blackpool from the hospital.

The next day this second doctor came up and put four shillings in my hand. 'What's this for?' I asked. 'That is from Dr Rand. He had sixpence each way on a horse called Carey's Cottage and it won. It was the name, you see, initials CC.'

Maintaining our dubious record of drawing in all our semi-final matches at Hillsborough, we only managed to scrape a 1-1 draw with York, Vic Keeble getting the all important goal that took the tie to Roker Park. There, ahead from the third minute, we made no mistake in the replay, running out 2-0 victors with White

Alec Mutch was a long-serving physio and assistant trainer.

and Keeble scoring the goals. And so we were back at Wembley, itching to get at Don Revie and Manchester City who had beaten Sunderland in the other semi.

We were then faced with a massive backlog of matches and a daunting ten games in twenty-three days. Even with Milburn out of the side with a groin strain, we began to get into some sort of rhythm by beating Everton 2-0, and sentencing Sheffield Wednesday to a swift return to the lower division with a 5-0 hammering. Over the Easter period, we recorded our first trio of wins since 1907.

In a game against Chelsea, Jackie Milburn was stood down as Livingstone persisted with his experimental process. 'We shall make changes regularly over the coming rush of matches,' he said, 'in order to give men a rest and to seek the most effective line-up for Wembley,' In effect, what he was doing was creating uncertainty in the minds of all the players, none of whom knew if his name would be on the team-sheet for any given match. It was a recipe for suspicion and unrest within a side that had once thrived on camaraderie.

We played a Blackpool side that had trounced Manchester City, our Cup opponents, 6-1 the previous week. Ivor Broadis was brought in for that game, but already knew that he didn't figure in Newcastle's Cup plans. A few days earlier he had seen his name on the top of a list in the office – the list was headed 'Open for Transfer'.

The match against Blackpool was drawn 1-1, but our fans were more interested in the postcards that were distributed at the turnstiles. Once filled in with names and addresses, the cards were to be used in a massive lottery to decide who was to get Cup Final tickets. If that was to prove an administrative pain for the board, it was nothing to the headache we players gave them as we trooped off the St James' pitch after the final whistle, demanding a substantial increase in our personal allocation of Cup Final tickets.

On Tuesday 29th April, the headline on the front page of the *Newcastle Journal* announced:

'Directors Say: Press Your Demands and We Play Reserve Side.'

Hadn't we heard that threat before? The board were trying to stick to an FA ruling that only *twelve* tickets be allocated to players. This had come about because of irregularities concerning the distribution of Cup Final tickets by Newcastle United and Arsenal in 1952.

As in 1951 and '52, the Newcastle United board had another eve-of-Final

I was still enjoying my football at United in spite of what was going on around me.

crisis to overcome, but even the ticket issue was nothing to what had been happening behind closed doors at Gallowgate. Livingstone had chosen *his* Cup Final team and presented it to the board ten days before the game. There was an uproar from the directors when it was noticed that the name of Milburn was *not* included. The manager's forward line read: White, Davies, Keeble, Hannah and Mitchell.

If Livingstone's stock had ever reached any great heights within the boardroom, it definitely fell far below zero with his proposal to send a Newcastle United team to Wembley without Jackie Milburn. The manager's selection was summarily despatched to the waste-paper basket and, within forty-eight hours, Livingstone himself was banished from his own office into the cubby hole set aside for match-day referees.

No mention was made to the press about the possible omission of Milburn, and as we left for Brighton prior to the last League game of the season at White Hart Lane, the following Cup Final team was announced: Simpson, Cowell, Batty, Scoular, Stokoe, Crowe, Milburn, Davies, Keeble, Hannah and Mitchell. Spurs, who still needed one more point to avoid relegation, dropped full-back Alf Ramsey in favour of Charlie Withers.

For me, this was the most disappointing day of my life. During the game I went for a fifty-fifty ball with Harry Clarke and fell awkwardly, spraining my ankle in the process. As I hobbled off that field assisted by Norman Smith I feared the worst.

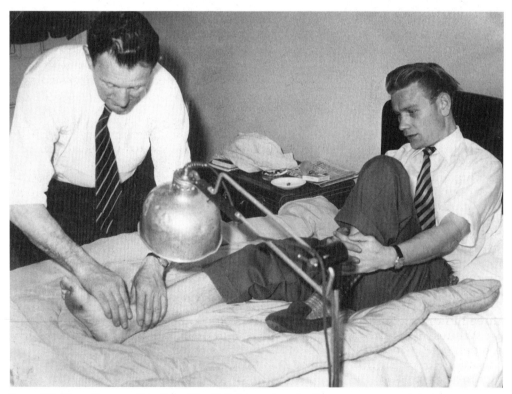

I couldn't wait to get back to the Brighton hotel where I was treated by an expert physio and masseur, Sam Cowan, attached to the Sussex County Cricket Club.

Prior to me being injured, the team had visited a Brighton craftsman who showed us the tricks of his trade. But what was he making? Could it be collars for shirts? I have forgotten. Back left: Jackie Milburn, Jimmy Scoular, Bob Cowell, Vic Keeble, George Hannah, Ron Simpson, Len White, Bob Stokoe, Ron Batty and me.

For three days Sam Cowan worked on the ankle using every known treatment, but all to no avail. Norman Smith sent me out for a short work-out on the Friday, the day before the Final, but the ankle was still very stiff and puffy. Stan Seymour had asked me for a decision by mid-afternoon. After turning and kicking the ball, Norman said: 'It's still not right, is it, Charlie?' Just then Jackie Milburn waved me over to where he was standing. He leaned over and whispered: 'You can still play, Charlie. Me and the rest of the lads will 'carry' you if you break down.' But I knew it wasn't right, and told Seymour. Tom Casey had already joined the party on Wednesday at the Royal Albion Hotel in Brighton. After a season where I had been more or less a regular first-team choice, it was galling to accept that I would be the one sitting on the touchline when all my mates were out there on the park, playing their hearts out.

But mine wasn't the only drama being enacted that fateful week more than three hundred miles away from Tyneside. Reg Davies came back to the hotel on Wednesday night looking very flushed and obviously running a temperature. A local GP was called in and he diagnosed laryngitis. A thermometer confirmed a temperature of 102, and poor Reg was immediately confined to his bed.

Next day it was announced that Len White would play outside-right at Wembley, with Jackie Milburn switching to inside-right. Lennie, so disappointed at being dropped from Livingstone's original selection, didn't know whether to be elated at getting into the team, or sorry for Reg Davies missing out at the last minute.

It was galling having to visit Reg Davies in hospital with our two replacements: Tom Casey and Len White. It was difficult to tell which pair were the most dismayed: Reg and I for missing out on a Cup Final, or Tom and Lennie for getting in through the back-door, as it were.

Five of that 1955 chosen FA Cup team who came back together at St James' Park in 1990: Bob Stokoe, Bob Cowell, Ronnie Simpson, me and Reg Davies who had travelled all the way back from Australia for the get-together.

On the Thursday night, Don Revie, Manchester City's centre-forward, was awarded 'Footballer of the Year', but paid tribute to his team-mates, saying: 'Without their help I would not be here, and though Manchester City football has been called the 'Revie Plan', it is a plan of all the lads.'

Don Revie is seen 4th right standing between Jackie Milburn and Nat Lofthouse, in what proved to be Milburn's last game for England against Denmark in Copenhagen. Fourth left is Bill McGarry who later managed Newcastle United. England won the match 5-1 with goals from Lofthouse (2), Revie (2) and Bradford.

Eleven Newcastle United wives and one girlfriend (Tommy Casey wasn't married) left Newcastle on the Friday night for London. They were in good company – 15,000 Geordies followed their team to Wembley, 9000 of them by rail, among them Matty Heslop of Gateshead sporting an eighteen-inch black and white topper, decorated with photographs of all the players.

Laura Milburn was the first of the players' wives off the train at Kings Cross, and when asked to predict the result, she tipped Newcastle to win 3-1. Bob Mitchell's wife was taking no chances and carried a lucky piece of coal in her handbag, while Elsie Cowell stuck with her familiar Cornish Pixie. 'It's brought me luck so far,' she said.

Elsie Cowell's maiden name was Prior, and the family lived in Duke Street, Ashington, named after the wealthy Duke of Portland who lived in nearby Bothal Castle and owned most of Ashington's land. Elsie's father, George, was a professional footballer for Sheffield Wednesday and Watford, and her brother Ken Prior played at outside left for Newcastle United in the late 1950s. Ken later became both a player and manager of Ashington FC.

At ten minutes to three on Saturday 7th May 1955 the teams walked out on the Wembley arena to be presented to royalty, Newcastle led by skipper Jimmy Scoular.

The Duke of Edinburgh meets a true Scot in the shape of Bobby Mitchell. The Duke and Jackie Milburn were to meet up again in the 1980s when Wor Jackie was given the Freedom of the City of Newcastle and Prince Philip presented Jackie with a sword.

Reg Davies and I, unnoticed by the crowd, quietly took our places on the bench. Throughout the Cup Final I was wearing a glum expression and a mackintosh only purchased days before in a Brighton shop. That coat was to feature a lot in the Sunday papers.

As a match, the 1955 Cup Final was very nearly a fiasco for the 100,000 spectators, despite four great goals. The game flared immediately when Jackie Milburn, left completely unguarded, flicked his head at a Len White right-wing corner kick, the ball whipped past Bert Trautman's outstretched right arm, dipped under the crossbar, and we had as good as won the Cup in only 45 seconds. After this unforgettable start, Jackie Milburn was never seen in the game.

Trautman easily deals with a Milburn challenge. As a spectacle, the Final was spoilt when, in the eighteenth minute, at precisely the same time and spot as Wally Barnes had been injured in 1952, Jimmy Meadows, chasing the ghost of Bobby Mitchell, over-reached himself and wrenched his knee and lower-leg ligaments, sustaining an injury that was to put him in plaster for six weeks. During the game I had to sit on the touchline knowing that I should have been out there with the lads.

The ten men of Manchester equalised just before the interval when Johnstone headed in a short pass from Hayes. The half-time whistle went with only one team playing cultured, stylish football – that team was Manchester City.

Don Revie closes in on Simpson's goal.

And yet by the fifty-eighth minute the game was all over bar the shouting, United having taken the lead with a goal from an impossible angle scored by Mitch, followed by another from George Hannah. After that, we played the game at walking pace before bursting forward to test Bert Trautman the German 'keeper who did well to keep the score down to 3-1.

The last captain of Newcastle to be handed the FA Cup was Jimmy Scoular. After the match, the Queen turned to Stan Seymour and said: 'You've broken a record, haven't you?'

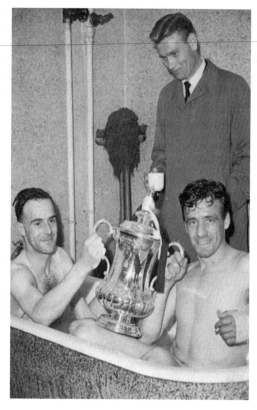

As Scoular was hoisted shoulder height, it was noticeable that the Newcastle manager Livingstone was nowhere to be seen. His place in the front line was taken by Norman Smith. Indeed, Newcastle United's three Wembley wins of the 1950s made wondrous soccer history, and I for one was proud to have played a part in it. But it was disappointing not being on the pitch to celebrate with my mates holding the Cup. For me, it was even more galling back in the dressing-room, watching the two Ronnies, Simpson and Batty, drinking champagne from the silver Cup while I drank cold tea from a china tea-cup.

THE QUEEN KNEW IT WAS CUP RECORD

Newcastle's five Wembley wins

"YOU have broken a record." That was The Queen's remark to Mr. Stan Seymour, chairman of Newcastle United, as the final whistle blew in Wembley Stadium yesterday afternoon.

The Queen and the Duke of Edinburgh — who must have supported United, for he once commanded the frigate Magpie—knew that United, conquerors of Manchester City, now hold every Wembley Cup Final record.

That Jackie Milburn goal in record time ensured that his name would go down in history as an all-time great.

Footballers' wives in the 1950s were always kept in the background. Not for them the catwalk or the 'Posh Spice' image. The women tended to shun the limelight, content to blossom forth on Cup Final day, as seen here in 1955. From left: Joyce Scoular, Elsie Cowell, Mrs Vic Keeble (in front), Belle Mitchell, Laura Milburn, Jean Stokoe, Lily Batty, June Hannah, Joyce White and Rosemary Simpson.

HOME WITH THE CUP
MAGPIES WILL GET 500,000 WELCOME

That was the banner headline in the *Sunday Sun*. Here is the rest of the column:

'Jamming the streets of Newcastle tomorrow will be half a million people – cheering themselves frantic in a great welcome home to United's players, who by their Cup victory over Manchester City, won a record that 50 years of football heralds as a glorious achievement. For Newcastle United have won the Cup for the *third* time in five years. But yesterday the city was as quiet as on a Sunday afternoon. Everybody seemed either at Wembley or at home, gazing intently at TV sets or listening excitedly to the sound broadcast of the match.

'Fourteen thousand fans followed the Magpies to London to cheer them to victory. And – a few minutes after the final whistle – Newcastle rocked with the cries of people who rushed from houses and shops: "The lads have done it again." Huge black and white banners were unfurled from stores.

'Tomorrow, the boys will be home. The engine of their train will announce proudly: "Newcastle United 'Howay'." And as the team enters the city they will have no difficulty with the traffic. For there will be no other traffic – all will be banned to admit a motor-coach sporting the colours of Newcastle United, Cup held high on the roof where the players will sit to receive thousands of pats and handshakes.

'Last night the club held a celebration dinner at the Savoy Hotel in London. It was Newcastle's sixth FA Cup win and their fifth at Wembley. Manchester City – fighting gamely with ten men – could not break the Tynesiders' attack. United put on two goals after a challenging equaliser. They were worthy winners. City agreed – "There's no doubt the better team won," said skipper Roy Paul. "But I think substitutes should be allowed for injured players in such an important game."

'A crowd of 100,000 saw the match. Receipts were £49,881. Before the game spivs were selling 3s 6d tickets for up to £4 each and 15s tickets for £8.'

As skipper Jimmy Scoular was hauled aloft, a rather embarrassed Dougald Livingstone managed to get into the picture at last. Little did any of the 50,000 United fans who packed St James' Park realise it, but this would be the last time in the 20th century that the FA Cup would be paraded in front of them by a victorious Newcastle United team.

IN MEMORY OF
JACKIE MILBURN

By Mike Kirkup

To try to capture the essence of Jackie Milburn's life in thirty minutes was clearly an impossibility for Eamonn Andrews and his programme 'This is Your Life', back in December 1981. And it was an equally daunting task when I set out, first of all to write a musical, then later a comprehensive biography of the great man, called 'Jackie Milburn in Black and White'.

The names of Milburn and Newcastle United are synonymous and there are few citizens of the 'toon' who can claim to have done so much for the team and the region as the man who wore the number-nine black and white striped shirt in the years following World War Two.

The Milburn connection, for me, had all begun way back in July 1988. I had decided to write a musical based on the life of John Edward Thompson (JET) Milburn, and managed to track the great man down to his house in Bothal Terrace, Ashington. Wor Jackie was living only a few yards from where he was born. During his footballing career with Newcastle United and England, he had travelled to the far corners of the world: Brazil, South Africa, Jackie's first cap in 1948 was gained in Ireland and the last of his thirteen England appearances was against Denmark in 1956. He said:

'I just couldn't wait to get back to Northumberland – the greatest place in the world. Aye, that's where I was born: 14 Sixth Row, Ashington. Presto's is there now. Overlooking the pityard into the tankey shed, that's where I was born. The tankeys used to puff, puff, puff all day and all night 'n' all, but you got used to it. I more or less lived there ... that was me Granny's house.'

Jackie Milburn was born on 11th May 1924 in the upstairs flat of his Granny Thompson's. Outside lay the cobbled colliery yard. The small houses were squeezed into a concertina terrace, overshadowed by the ever-rotating winding gear straddling a pit riddled with thin, deep shafts. A thousand feet below the ground, strong sinews of coal spread out in the nearby pits, the names of which rang out like bells at Sunday Worship: Shilbottle, Lynemouth, Linton, Pegswood, Woodhorn, Blackhill, Ellington, Whittle, Newbiggin, Broomhill, North Seaton, Longhirst Drift, and, at the heart of them all, Ashington, the biggest mining village in the world.

Opposite page: Ashington was a town built around a pit. The Sixth Row where Jackie was born is seen top left, almost in the pit-yard itself. Behind it are rows known simply be their numbers: 5th, 4th, 3rd, 2nd and 1st: the gaffers' street. Beyond the colliery rows you can see the pit heaps that dominated the town until the 1970s when they were eventually demolished.

Number 3 was a favourite among the tankey drivers at Ashington Pit. This photo was taken in 1947 when busy tankeys carried millions of tons of coal each year from the Ashington Group of Collieries which also included Woodhorn, Linton, Lynemouth and Ellington. Now only Ellington Pit remains as the last deep-shaft mine in the north of England.

It had been back in 1920 when Ashington Coal Company, which had acquired a reputation for taking a great interest in the miners' well being away from work, directed considerable funds towards the establishment of a Welfare Department embracing educational, sporting and leisure facilities. It was this sporting provision that was to turn the pit village of Ashington into a 'football factory' out of which dozens of local lads were to stumble from the pit cage into some of the greatest football teams of the day. The blue scars of the mine were in their blood, but so was football. And if you asked where their hearts and ambitions lay, hungry eyes would turn in the direction of the Tyne and Newcastle United. For that was the only escape from the mines. It was a straight choice: the pits or football – but only if you were good enough.

Milburn told me: 'I counted up one day, and I got as far as forty-seven Ashington lads who had made the grade into League football, and I mean First Division 'n' all – none of your lower League stuff.'

And it was only the pits or football for one of Jackie's relatives: his second cousin, Jack Charlton, seen here bare-headed in centre of back row of pit trainees. Charlton was part of what was known as the Pit Training Scheme in 1950, but was only at the colliery for about six months when he was spotted by a Leeds United scout and taken down to Elland Road.

During our interview, the question arose as to where the musical play might begin – at which point in Milburn's life, that is. 'Whey, man, there's only one place you can start: where it all began, with me walking up the Wembley steps to get me first FA Cup winner's medals from the King in 1951.'

That interview lasted the best part of three hours as Milburn weaved his way through a life studded with glittering highlights. I eventually ran out of audio tapes and had to leave, promising to return at a later date. Alas, it was the last time I saw Jackie Milburn alive. Within a few months this once heavy smoker lay dead from lung cancer.

Another local lad managed to get away from the pits and make a name for himself as a prolific goalscorer, both for Aberdeen and Newcastle United. Bobby Cummings is seen here with Charlie Crowe at Woodhorn Colliery Museum in 1996 beside what is definitely – in my opinion – the best of the *three* Milburn statues in existence. If you think it looks familiar, it is because this version – the work of local sculptor Tom Maley – once stood in the concourse of St James' Park for about two years in the late 1990s. Incredibly, the Newcastle United board failed to come up with the necessary money needed to cast the statue in bronze and it now languishes in the sculptor's back garden in Longhirst Village. (Tom Maley's statue of Wilf Mannion now holds pride of place at the Riverside Stadium.)

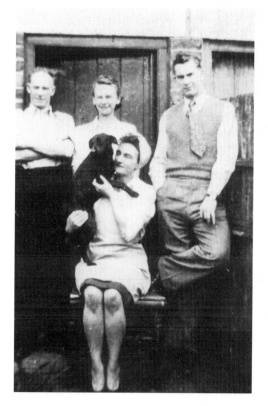

Here we see Jackie as a youth with his father Alec and sister Jean. His mother Nance is seated in front with the family pet dog, Vic. See the rough-and-ready railings that separated this front garden in the Sixth Row from next door. Jackie's father, was a cutterman down Ashington Pit.

Each colliery house was, in effect, a tied cottage. Once a man accepted the house he was shackled to the Coal Company for life, little more than a serf. None of the miners' houses had indoor plumbing of any kind, and water was drawn from a communal tap in the backstreet.

Wor Jackie shook the hands of VIPs all through his footballing career. He is seen here (with a broken wrist) at Bolton's Burnden Park being introduced to Field Marshall Montgomery. On Jackie's left is another Ashington lad who escaped the pits, Dougie Graham.

Jackie Milburn was not alone in being a Newcastle United smoker. The team were even given cigarettes by the management as a perk. Here he is at St James' Park in 1959 watching a game from the bench. On left is a young Bobby Moncur, destined to guide United to an Inter City Fairs Cup success – the last trophy to be won by Newcastle.

My script for the musical 'Wor Jackie' went on to win a substantial cash award from London Weekend Television's Plays on Stage competition, and the resulting TV documentary 'JET', which I wrote for Tyne Tees Television, won for them the Royal Television Institute's Rose Bowl for Best Regional Programme of 1989. The £12,000 prize went to the Northumberland Theatre Company to enable them to go on tour the following Spring.

Here is the cover of the programme for 'Wor Jackie'. One of the judges who thought that 'Wor Jackie' was a marvellous musical was Dame Judy Dench. When I asked her at the presentation at the Savoy Hotel in December 1988 if she had only voted for the play out of sympathy for the main character who had only been dead a couple of months, she insisted: 'I voted for the musical on merit. I thought that it would make an excellent stage production.' Fellow judge, actor Tim Piggot Smith, interjected: 'Yes, but I would take a pair of scissors to it if I was you – it is far too long.' I took his advice.

"Wor Jackie"

Jackie Milburn! He's .....
Venerable Bede
in a black 'n' white strip,
Saint Cuthbert
in an England cap, and
Saint Aidan
in a pair of size six football
boots, all rolled into one.

He's .....
Bonnier than Bobby Shaftoe.
Bigger than the Lambton Worm.

Whey ..... the man's a legend.

These are some of the words that did survive the scissors into the final production where I likened Milburn to Bede, Cuthbert and Aidan, three North East saints that I was to return to when writing the libretto of 'With the Ebb and the Flow'; set to music by Derek Hobbs, it tells the story of how the Venerable Bede did so much for the region. Rather like Jackie Milburn, I suppose.

In between all that, I had been asked to write a biography on Milburn's life for publishers Stanley Paul of London, a branch of what is now Random Century. I realised that it was time to start putting money back into Milburn's name, so I donated most of the royalties from this book into opening a charity named the Jackie Milburn Memorial Trust Fund for disadvantaged North East

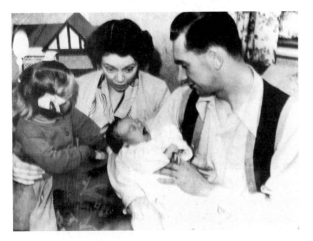

children. I later wrote a TV documentary: 'JET – a Tribute to Jackie Milburn' which was screened on Tyne Tees Television in 1989 and was also made into a video.

Jackie Milburn met his Scottish-born wife Laura while the team were staying at a hotel near Luton. He was very much a family man, being very proud of his two girls Linda and Betty (seen here) and his son Jack junior who came along later.

Jackie always said that Laura did not take much interest in football – and that was the way he liked it. This is Laura's first visit to a match – the 1951 FA Cup Final. Seconds after this photo was taken, someone pinched Laura's scarf from her neck as a souvenir.

Whatever Jackie Milburn was doing, he always took time out to help and befriend children, as seen in this photo from around 1952. It was this rapport with children that led me to believe that a charity in his name, linked to local children, might have met with his approval.

During the run of the musical at Newcastle Playhouse, I had struck up a friendship with many of Milburn's former team mates who became trustees of the Fund. They are seen here at the launch of Jackie's biography at St James' Park in 1990. From left: Bobby Cowell, Frank Brennan, Charlie Crowe, myself and George Luke.

The first recipient of the award was a thirteen-year-old Downes Syndrome lad, Paul Stearman of Cramlington. The then directors of Newcastle United, Gordon McKeag and Peter Mallinger, really went to town in their lavish hospitality for Paul and his family, and a good selection of United's players from then (1990) turned out to make it a memorable day for young Paul, seen here with myself, club chairman Gordon McKeag and Charlie.

Charlie Crowe was a good friend of Newcastle's then vice chairman Peter Mallinger, and it was Peter who – when he couldn't get up to Newcastle from his home town of Leicester – passed on three of his tickets for the directors' box on matchdays at St James'. Charlie rotated the tickets between Frank Brennan, one of his pals … and me. And that is how I found myself sitting in the luxury of the directors' box, next to legends like Charlie and Big Frank. At that time Ida Harvey, Joe's widow, was also allotted three tickets, two of which went to Bobby Cowell and his wife Elsie.

Those Saturdays, when I received the invitation phone call from Charlie, provided me with some great moments although, in that 1989/90 season, Newcastle United did not have a great team – they didn't even have a good team. They were in the doldrums and in the lower half of the old Second Division, entertaining teams like Port Vale and Hull – not exactly mouth-watering fixtures.

It was on 17th March 1990 that Gordon McKeag welcomed Laura Milburn to open the stand named in her late husband's honour. This is what Gordon wrote in the programme:

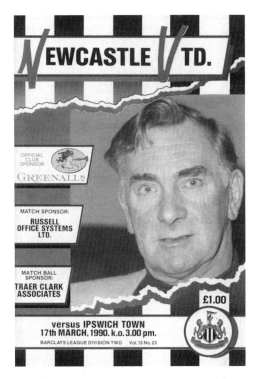

'I am delighted to welcome Mrs Laura Milburn to St James' Park today and I am very pleased that she has agreed to open the new Milburn Stand … which is a fitting and lasting tribute to the legendary Jackie Milburn … it is no coincidence that the match against Ipswich Town has been chosen for this opening ceremony. Jackie Milburn was manager there from January 1963 to September 1964.'

The Milburns had always been used to having things named after them. In 1950 it was an exotic orchid that bore the name 'Jackie Milburn', given by a local horticulturist.

At noon on Saturdays, I would call for Charlie at his home near the Four Lane Ends and we'd catch the Metro into town. Charlie was recognised at every turn by old supporters, and he acknowledged them all with a smile and a friendly word. Once at St James' we'd climb those few steps to the main entrance where Charlie was invariably greeted by the uniformed man on the door like a long-lost friend. Inside the lobby would be Bobby Cowell, perhaps chatting to George Taylor, a Tyne Tees TV pundit and then acting as a PR man for United.

In another corner was Doug Weatherall (seen here between Cowell and Crowe at a Paul Joannou book launch) getting quotes for his *Daily Mail* column.

I just stood, open-mouthed, drinking in the fabulous atmosphere. About five minutes before kick-off, Frank Brennan would arrive, a broad smile creasing his craggy face. By then in his sixties, the rangy Scot still radiated a commanding presence that must have scared the living daylights out of opposing centre-forwards in the 1950s. Bobby Cowell was still as fiery as ever, always quick to pounce and air his views on something that he considered to be out of order, whether it be on the management side or on the pitch. What a formidable trio Crowe, Brennan and Cowell must have made on the park!

Watching the actual games, for me, was almost something of an anti-climax after the initial introductions in the foyer. Newcastle's captain then was Roy Aitken, their recently-acquired Scottish international, bought to bolster up a weak United defence. Aitken had a brilliant football brain, but his legs were often not up to the kick and rush tactics of many Second Division sides. Up front, Newcastle had the mighty Mickey Quinn who could turn on a tanner with his back to the opposition and produce a goal out of nothing. Curiously, he was not as adept when going forward.

BOBBY COWELL

FRANK BRENNAN

CHARLIE CROWE

IT WAS great to see three former Newcastle FA Cup giants at last Saturday's impressive third round victory over Derby County at St James's Park.

But I wonder if Bobby Cowell, Frank Brennan and Charlie Crowe realised that Saturday was 40 years to the day that Newcastle United embarked on the greatest run in the history of the FA Cup.

Just for the record

For on January 6, 1951, United beat Bury 4-1 in the third round before a 33,944 St James's Park crowd, who paid £3,300 to set the ball rolling.

Crowe and Cowell both played that day with Brennan coming into the team for the fifth round victory over Stoke City.

The Cup was won that year. And the following year. And just for good measure in 1955 as well.

That record will never surely be bettered. And while Saturday could prove to be the turning point for Newcastle United, there isn't a snowball's chance in hell of that run which started 40 years ago being repeated.

This is what the *Football Chronicle* had to say about the trio in January 1991. Needless to say, Newcastle did not go on to win the FA Cup in 1991 … or since.

Lee Clark, Micky Quinn and Roy Aitken made sure it was a day that Paul Stearman would remember for the rest of his life. One of the reasons that Paul was chosen for the Milburn award was because of his sporting success when taking part in the 1989 Special Games.

And that was Newcastle United at the beginning of the 1990s, managed by the 'bald eagle' himself, Jim Smith. Over the next year or so, Newcastle hovered dangerously close to the wrong end of the table. Managers came and went. Ossie Ardiles was brought in, but his management skills never threatened to match his on-the-pitch brilliance. Off the pitch there were still boardroom wranglings as Gordon McKeag and John Hall attempted to form an uneasy alliance. And then came Kevin Keegan, and it was as though a cloud had been lifted from St James' Park as the inspired Magpies flew to promotion and the newly-formed Premier League. Newcastle United were where the fans knew they belonged: back in the big time.

John Hall's trump card was played when he ushered Kevin Keegan into a packed press conference and announced that the charismatic Kevin was to be United's new manager. This seemingly was also the first time Ossie Ardiles had heard anything about it. Photo shows from left: Albert Stubbins, Charlie Crowe, Sir John Hall, Kevin Keegan, Newcastle's Lord Mayor and Frank Brennan.

In a Newcastle United programme in October 1992 Kevin Keegan had this to say under the heading 'Our aim is to become another Liverpool and dominate football.'

'I don't think that there is any doubt now that we are the biggest club outside the Premier League. We are playing Premier football, we have Premier players and have crowds bigger than the majority of Premier League clubs.

'Our aim is to become another Liverpool and dominate football. There is something happening here that is not happening anywhere else – full grounds every week. We are turning people away. Locking fans out. I feel sorry for them because some of them have been supporting this club when it wasn't worthy of support, and now, unfortunately, they cannot get in. You cannot expect to come out of the Strawberry pub at five to three and get into the ground any more.'

Unfortunately, neither I nor my new-found friends were allowed to share in United's renaissance. Peter Mallinger relinquished his position on the Newcastle board to take over the reins at Kettering Town, so Charlie was unable to get tickets. Sadly, Bobby Cowell and Frank Brennan died within a year of each other, leaving Charlie Crowe as the sole survivor on Tyneside of that victorious 1951 FA Cup side. (Tommy Walker is living near Manchester).

But the Milburn Trust Fund carries on, going from strength to strength as the list of award recipients grows over the years. In 1993, by pure coincidence, it was seven-year-old Nikky Milburn who benefited from his namesake's Milburn Trust award. Nikky, who comes from Prudhoe, Northumberland, suffers from the rare disease Ehlers-Danlos Syndrome which means that he cannot mix or play football with other youngsters.

In 1994 we made a double award, first to Zoe Hurcombe (2nd left) of Heaton Manor School, who suffers from Charcol-Marle-Tooth Disease, who was presented with a cheque for £250 plus a holiday at Parkdean Holidays in Perth. That same day,

senior physiotherapist Michelle Mander (2nd right) was given a cheque for £250 for the Tyneside Challenge Club which was raising funds to send wheelchair-bound children from Pendower Hall Special School, on holiday to Disneyworld, Florida.

Charlie hands over vital equipment in 1995 to the children of Windsor First School, Newbiggin by the Sea, as head Mrs Laura Cunningham looks on.

At a cabaret dance to raise money for the Fund in 1999 at Newbiggin Leisure Centre, we persuaded Mrs Laura Milburn (on left) and Charlie to hand over a £250 cheque and a signed Newcastle United shirt to one of the teachers at the Riverbank Special Department, attached to Hirst High School, Ashington, so that they could raffle it for their own funds.

Charlie was on hand to hand over a donation to the St Oswald's Hospice in Gosforth. Mitsubishi dealers Pearson Motors of Benton raised £500 by offering people the chance to have their photographs

taken with the FA Cup. Here Penelope Jackson of St Oswald's Jigsaw appeal receives the cheque with Debra Stevens of Pearsons.

Now let Charlie's wife Ruth Crowe have the last word.

'After the '55 Final we all went back to the Savoy for a celebration dinner, just as Newcastle had done each time they'd won. Charlie was *still* wearing that mac, and he and I are seen here with Newcastle's Town Clerk and Lord Mayor, John Atkinson.

'Inside, I found myself sitting next to Tommy Casey who had come into the side at the last minute for Charlie. Well, Tommy was absolutely distraught, and in a strong Irish accent he said: "Oh, Ruth, Ah feel really bad about me havin' this medal when sure it should have been Charlie himself who should be after havin' it."

'He went on and on so much that, in the end, I said: "All right then, Tommy, let's have the bloody thing!" But Newcastle minted another one for Charlie and Reg Davies after we came home, so we got a medal anyway.

'I recall that in 1951 at the Savoy I had sat next to Frank Brennan, God bless him, who was tucking into some giant asparagus tips, eating the stalk and everything, singing at the top of his voice, "Figaro! Figaro!" And that was *before* he'd had a drink! They were happy happy times.'

Acknowledgements

Thanks to Jean Leithead (Jackie Milburn's sister) and Elsie Cowell for access to their personal scrapbooks and albums. To Neil Dunnett for permission to use Jackie Laws' NCB photos from his late father Eric's 1950 Hirst East School project. To John Ferguson and Neil Atkinson for *Wor Jackie* calligraphy and programme photo, respectively. To Ashington photographers Reuben Daglish, Jack Wallace and Mike Parker; plus Palmers Photography of Newcastle. To the Newcastle Football Chronicle, Newcastle Journal and Evening Chronicle, Sunday Sun, Sunday Pictorial, The People, Sunday Dispatch, News Chronicle, News of the World, Daily Express, Sunday Express, Daily Mirror and Daily Mail, for permission to use various articles and photos; and to other newspapers where we were unable to trace the source.

Grateful thanks to Newcastle United FC board members past and present, and club historian, Paul Joannou. Also to publishers Stanley Paul for permission to use extracts from Jackie Milburn's *Golden Goals*, published in 1957, and Mike Kirkup's book *Jackie Milburn in Black and White*, published in 1990. And to Newcastle City Library for access to newspaper records from the 1950s. Also to Mrs Lorna Kirkup for her meticulous typing of the manuscript.

Newcastle United defend against a Chelsea free-kick at Stamford Bridge in the early 1950s.

Charlie Crowe was given a free transfer from Newcastle United in 1957, and after talks with Mansfield's manager, Charlie Mitten, he went to the Third Division side as their captain. A bad injury a year later put him out of the game and he was offered the manager's job at Whitley Bay who were then at the bottom of the Northern League. While there he signed on John Mitten, Charlie's son. Charlie Mitten by then was manager of Newcastle United. He had asked Charlie Crowe to become his head coach at St James', but there was a difference of opinion about salary.

Whitley Bay's team seen here in 1959 was from back left: H. Ross (trainer), Oakley, Newham, Edgar, Walton, Robson, Browell and Charlie. Front: Stoker, Johnson, Duffy, Bell and Mitten.

The Charlie Crowe Appeal
charliecroweappeal.com